PJ 5129. G6 GOR

The Jewish King Lear

The Jewish King Lear:
A Comedy in America

Jacob Gordin

Translated by Ruth Gay

With Notes and Essays by
Ruth Gay and Sophie Glazer

Yale University Press   New Haven & London

Frontispiece: Jacob Gordin. (Archives of the YIVO Institute for Jewish Research)

Copyright © 2007 by Ruth Gay and Sophie Glazer.

Designed by James J. Johnson and set in Galliard Roman by Keystone Typesetting, Inc.
Printed in the United States of America by Edwards Brothers, Ann Arbor, Michigan.

Library of Congress Cataloging-in-Publication Data

Gordin, Jacob, 1853–1909.
[Der Yudisher Kenig Lir. English]
The Jewish King Lear : A comedy in America / Jacob Gordin ; translated by Ruth Gay : with
notes and essays by Ruth Gay and Sophie Glazer. — 1st ed.
p. cm.
Includes bibliographical references and index.
ISBN 978-0-300-10875-0 (alk. paper)

I. Gay, Ruth. II. Title.
PJ5129.G6Y913 2007
839'.123—dc22   2006037325

A catalogue record for this book is available from the British Library.

The paper in this book meets the guidelines for permanence and durability of the Committee on
Production Guidelines for Book Longevity of the Council on Library Resources.

10 9 8 7 6 5 4 3 2 1

For
Alan Astrow, Jerome Groopman, Jeffrey Tepler, and Eric Feldman

Contents

Acknowledgments

The authors would like to express their appreciation to the staff of the YIVO Archives, where the original manuscript of *The Jewish King Lear* is now located. We are particularly grateful to Krysia Fisher and Jesse Aaron Cohen for their assistance with the photographs for this book, to Fruma Mohrer, head of the archives, and to Chana Mlotek for her help in deciphering the indecipherable. We also applaud the Yiddish Book Center for their invaluable work in saving the literature of a dying tongue from extinction.

It was a pleasure to meet (through the Internet) Beth Kaplan, the great-granddaughter of Jacob Gordin. She is herself in the process of publishing a biography of Gordin and kindly shared an early draft with us. Our publisher, Jonathan Brent, demonstrated an admirable open-mindedness to this venture, and we are also obliged to Victor Bers for his interest in this rather unusual project.

Sarah Glazer Khedouri took charge of the illustrations for this book, Lama Al-Aswad provided invaluable medical advice, and we are indebted as well to the friendly involvement and useful suggestions of Doron Ben-Atar, Clara Cohen, Elizabeth Glazer, Shirley Gorenstein, Eli Khedouri, and David Rogow. Joel Berkowitz provided invaluable insights in his learned reading of the manuscript. As always, Peter Gay supported the project from beginning to end.

Introduction

The Text of *The Jewish King Lear*

The original text of *The Jewish King Lear*—here appearing in print for the first time—was probably never performed. The beloved and profoundly influential staple of the Yiddish stage known as *The Jewish King Lear* was in fact a hybrid production: Jacob Gordin's original text, as published here, was purchased by the actor-manager Jacob Adler, who revised it extensively. Adler's charismatic presence in the title role virtually guaranteed its success, and his revisions demonstrated his keen eye for what worked on stage. Adler stripped away a problematic final scene, with a provocative background of Christian music; he tactfully eliminated Gordin's attack on musical interludes; he toned down the defiance, piled on the pathos, and created a lasting hit.

The Jewish King Lear remained in Adler's repertory for thirty years after its premiere in 1892—but what audiences saw was Adler's version. There is no record at all that Gordin's play was ever performed as he wrote it or that the text was ever published. The play did appear in print in Warsaw as early as 1898, but it was a pirated edition presumably taken from a prompter's script of the Adler version and was totally unauthorized by Gordin. It was reprinted in 1907 shortly before Gordin's death. A number of manuscript copies of the play in the YIVO library, one from as early as 1894, are all in accord with the printed version. These seem to be fair copies of performance texts. In addition, a copy of the printed 1898 edition is in the Adler papers at the YIVO library with markings on it presumably made by Adler himself. Since we know that Gordin was a tiger in defending his prose from actors' improvisations — a widespread custom at the time — we can only assume that Adler, with his brilliant instinct for what worked on the stage and his finely honed judgment for what moved his audience, must have prevailed in a struggle between the two men. Adler's adaptation of Gordin's work ran for decades, but Gordin's original play, his idiosyncratic, passionate, iconoclastic play, has remained unperformed and unpublished, until now.

The Two King Lears: Shakespeare and Gordin

Shakespeare's *King Lear* combined the plot elements of a folktale and a historic tragedy. The history tells of an ancient British king and his long-forgotten defeat; it is the other element of *Lear*, the folktale, which Gordin recognized as timeless. In this tale, a king unwisely demands that each of his three daughters tell him how much she loves him: he believes the extravagant protestations of his sycophantic older daughters and banishes his honest youngest child.

As Shakespeare tells it, the king foolishly divides his kingdom between the older daughters, imagining that they will love him and honor him after he has relinquished his wealth and power. Once stripped of his crown, however, he finds that he is merely an encumbrance to them. Accompanied only by an honest old friend and a truth-telling fool, he leaves his daughters' grudging hospitality to wander penniless in the cold world he once ruled. His loving younger daughter returns to succor him, but the political machinations of his two power-hungry daughters lead ultimately to his death and to that of his beloved child.

Shakespeare's *King Lear* is only apparently about ancient Britain: the narrative, as Gordin saw, examined the forever troubling moment when a powerful patriarch relinquishes his authority to a younger generation. In Gordin's view, this moment extended far beyond the familial politics of love and power: this tale reflected the far more complex struggle taking place in the families of his audience, families in which parental power was already compromised by the exigencies of the immigrant experience. American-born children challenged the authority of their immigrant parents in countless ways; the children's easy mastery of the language in which their parents struggled and their confident understanding of the new culture which baffled their parents led these American-born offspring to reject the notion that their parents had anything to teach them. To

Gordin's audience, the sufferings of parents whose children no longer honor them was a powerful theme indeed.

Gordin's play was set in 1890, in Vilna, in the house of a prosperous merchant named Dovidl Moysheles. The play opens as Dovidl lavishly, generously celebrates Purim with his large family, including his two married daughters, Etele and Gitele, and his unmarried youngest daughter, Taybele. Also present, at Taybele's invitation, is her tutor, Yaffe, the Enlightened German Jew who serves as the author's voice. Although Purim custom includes the exchange of modest plates of sweets, Dovidl instead gives rich gifts of diamonds to his daughters. The two older daughters accept their jewels with flattering thanks, but his gift is refused by Taybele, who claims she has no need of such adornment. Dovidl announces that he has decided to spend his remaining years in the land of Israel in prayer and study, and that he is giving his fortune to his oldest son-in-law to administer. His wife, his shrewd servant, who plays the fool, and his daughter Taybele are filled with foreboding. When Taybele objects, Dovidl storms at her and sends her away. Yaffe then rises to issue this warning: "Reb Dovidl, I do not know if you have heard of the world-famous writer Shakespeare. Among his works is a drama with the title *King Lear*. The old king, like you, divided his kingdom and also like you sent away the loving daughter who told him the truth. Oh, how dearly he paid for that! Yes, you are a Jewish King Lear! May God protect you from such an end as that to which King Lear came. May you be healthy and happy."

Dovidl blindly accepts the flattering assurances of his older daughters and their husbands only to learn, painfully, the truth of Yaffe's warning. He returns penniless from the land of Israel when his son-in-law stops his remittances, and he is reduced to living as an unwelcome guest in his own house. His daughter withholds food, starving him and his wife. His sight fails him, and in despair he leaves his house, accompanied only by his loyal servant, to beg his way around the world. It is only the love and skill of his youngest daughter, who has become an accomplished doctor, that restores his sight and sets matters right by the end of the play.

The Major Differences

There are a number of significant differences between Gordin's play and the performance text. One of the most remarkable occurs in the first act, where Gordin created an opportunity to lecture his audience severely on their debased taste for the musical interludes that customarily interrupted a serious drama. Gordin had long been accused of writing "dry" plays, without intervals of song and dance, and in *The Jewish King Lear* he addressed this criticism head-on by arranging for the arrival of Purim players at the end of the first act. They put on a traditional Purim play with song and dance to the immense enthusiasm of Dovidl and the rest of the guests. At the end, Dovidl turns to Yaffe and invites him to share in his delight. But, speaking in the voice of Gordin, Yaffe denounces the whole performance for its crudeness. In the stage version this scene was never played; instead, the guests at the feast sing as a chorus, and Yaffe, the exotic outsider, is invited to sing separately a song from his own tradition.

In the opening scene of the play, as the grandchildren are led in to offer their very formal good wishes, Adler devised a brilliant bit of stage business. His daughter Celia was two and a half years old when the play opened, and he arranged for her to appear as one of Etele's children. As she comes up to him, Adler lifts her high over his head while she lisps her very formal greeting: "Grandpa, may you live well over the next year together with Grandma and once again give presents."[1] As Celia Adler herself reported it, the moment totally melted the hearts of the audience.

At the end of the third act when Dovidl resolves to leave the cruel household of his daughter to go out as a beggar in the streets, Adler understood better than Gordin how to wring the most out of this scene. Gordin — and here this seems of a piece with his own proud nature — has Dovidl leave with his head high, saying, "Vivat the Jewish King Lear!" Adler, who understood the power of pathos on a Jewish audience, changed the scene; as he is about to leave, Dovidl imagines aloud his life as a beggar, hoping to find "good people" who will pity him. He leaves the stage in his new role saying, in a broken voice, "Give alms, give alms to the Jewish King Lear." According to contemporary accounts the stage would then be covered with coins rained down by an audience totally caught in the moment.

For Gordin the play was nothing less than a parable about the triumph of the Enlightenment and science over religion and superstition. This all comes to a climax in the last act of Gordin's original manuscript, when Taybele and Yaffe, both now doctors, operate on Dovidl to remove the cataracts that have blinded him. Here Gordin returns to his old passion and belief in universal brotherhood by opening the scene in the operating room with Yaffe complaining about the sound of singing from a church nearby. "That's what happens when they build a hospital near a Catholic church. It's a nuisance but to the devil with it." Taybele replies, presumably speaking for Gordin, "That singing isn't bothersome. Just the reverse. For the sick person it is surely pleasant. Ach — what an impression that singing makes now." The stage directions then call for several minutes of silence while the operation is performed. Presumably during this interval the Yiddish theater would have been filled with the music of the Mass. Adler excised this entire scene, probably reasoning that his Jewish audience, who saw the church in Russia as compliant in the periodic pogroms, was not yet ready to hear the sounds of a Mass with any sympathy.

When Dovidl awakes from the operation he sees the light not only physically but also philosophically and makes a passionate speech which sums up Gordin's message. This entire scene with Dovidl's speech was cut from all later versions of the play and was probably never staged by Adler despite the opportunity it gave him for a ringing theatrical moment. Instead the play ends on a note of reconciliation led by "the heretic" Yaffe, who says, ". . . let me be the first to extend my hand."

The Original Manuscript of *The Jewish King Lear*

This translation of the play is based on Gordin's handwritten manuscript, now among his papers in the YIVO archives. Gordin liked to write his plays in Russian schoolchildren's copybooks. There was one problem: when he came to the end of the copybook in which he wrote *Lear,* he had not quite finished the play. A search of the Gordin papers at YIVO failed to turn up any additional pages. It is also possible that Gordin never wrote down the last lines to his play: Gordin was known to appear at the theater with three acts of a four-act play completed and hastily improvise the last act on the spot. Similarly here — with the last pages of dialogue so obvious to him, he may not have bothered to put it down and may have just rehearsed the actors quickly at the last moment in the rather simple closing lines.

It is clear from the context that Gordin was within a page or two of ending the play and at this point the two versions — Gordin's original and the various performance texts — also began to converge. Despite Dovidl's fiery speech, his intention was not to break with the traditional life or to reject his religious sons-in-law. Rather, the effect of his new revelation is to make him more inclusive — to accept Taybele's wish to be "a useful

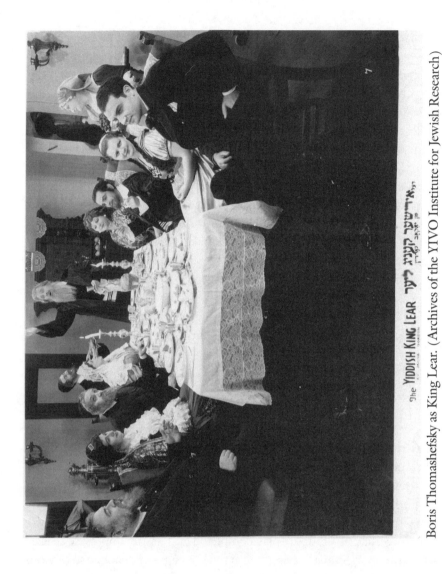

Boris Thomashefsky as King Lear. (Archives of the YIVO Institute for Jewish Research)

person" and also to accept his new heretic son-in-law for his scientific accomplishments and his noble heart.

Since both versions were moving to the same "happy ending" we have added on to Gordin's incomplete text a conclusion, assembled from the last pages of the dialogue in the other *Lear* manuscripts in the YIVO library collection. Although these are probably not Gordin's original words, we think they fulfill his intention, and they are certainly words that were heard in the theater.

This play, now more than a hundred years old, has a double force. On the one hand, it evokes the living passions of the period, secularism versus religion, the place of women in traditional Jewish society. But even as it appeared, what was still a source of struggle in the Old Country had already been realized in the new. The audience of the Yiddish theater was full of Taybeles. They were not doctors or scientists; they were hardworking independent women who could—and did—buy their own diamond earrings. Today the play survives not only in its antiquarian charm but also because its central themes—the relationship between parents and children and the more philosophical issues of secularism versus religion—are still alive and making headlines.

Adler continued to play the Lear role until the end of his life. Although disabled by a stroke in 1920 he could manage the first act of Lear, where he sits enthroned at the head of his table. He gave his last performance at a benefit in 1924 just two years before his death.

A decade later, *Lear* had a new incarnation under the auspices of the Works Project Administration. This admirable project of the New Deal was intended to support artists during the lean years of the Depression and included the actors of the Yiddish theater as well. Boris Thomashefsky was asked to head the Yiddish actors' project. He chose Gordin's *Jewish King Lear* as the work to be presented. It was offered free to audiences around New York in both Yiddish and English translation.

While it has not had a full production since then, the play surfaces from time to time in staged readings. We hope the publication of this new text will encourage the growing Yiddishist movement to look again at this still touching and witty play.

A Note on the Text

This translation was made directly from Jacob Gordin's handwritten manuscript and as such presented certain difficulties. Gordin's work is liberally encrusted with marginalia, interlineations, and afterthoughts. So tangled are the pages, so minute the interpolations and the addenda to interpolations, that some words are impossible to decipher.

There is also the problem of Yiddish expressions that lack English counterparts. "Baruch haba," we hear from Trytel — "Blessed is he who comes." This very routine welcome in Yiddish has no equivalent in English. "Vay iz mir," just as common, is usually translated literally as "Woe is me," which sounds far too formal and melodramatic. Many words growing out of the religious tradition have no exact English equivalent: "hairsplitting exegesis" doesn't really convey "pilpul"; "commentaries" is a little antiseptic as a translation for "Gemara"; "tsaddik" loses something when it becomes "holy man." For such words we have compromised; we retain the original in the text but urge the reader to consult the glossary.

This translation stays as close as possible to the literal meaning of Gordin's words. We have occasionally retained the original Yiddish expressions, if it seemed to us that they had some currency with the modern English speaker, and have retained speech rhythms that place our text somewhere between colloquial English and colloquial Yiddish. There is, we found, a fine line between the awkward locutions of absolute literalism and the anachronistic smoothness of idiomatic modern English. In making the choices we did we recreated as closely as possible the tone and flavor of Gordin's Yiddish, a language that fused theatricality with the simple, familiar expressions his audience used in their everyday life.

The Jewish King Lear

BY JACOB GORDIN

A Comedy in Four Acts

Dramatis Personae

Reb Dovidl Moysheles	*A rich Jew and a scholar*	*60 years old*
Khane Leah	*His wife*	*60 years old*
Etele	*His eldest daughter*	*30 years old*
Avrom Harif	*Her husband; a Misnagid*	*30 years old*
Gitele	*His second daughter*	*25 years old*
Moyshe Hasid	*Her husband*	*25 years old*
Taybele	*His third daughter*	*17 years old*
Trytel	*His servant*	*40 years old*
Herr Yaffe	*A student at the Rabbinical Academy*	*22 years old*

Purim players, guests, Hasidim
The action takes place in Vilna.

Act I

[*A large room in R. Dovidl's house. In the middle a long table covered with a white tablecloth. Khane Leah and Trytel are setting the table. He is jolly and a little drunk. Taybele (in a white apron) helps. On the table stand many large bottles of wine and brandy, glasses and goblets.*]

Khane Leah. Now it seems to me that everything is ready. Trytel, go and bring the Purim bread.

Trytel. Don't worry, Mistress, be without fear

The Purim bread will soon be here

With all my loyal wishes this year

From top to toe, good health, good cheer.

Truly mistress, may it come to pass

For you and your husband and your children and your children's children!

Taybele. [*Laughs.*] Ah! Trytel, you are talking in rhymes like a real wedding jester!

Trytel. I am neither a wedding jester nor a matchmaker, but also not a swindler. On Purim it's a very pious deed to get drunk. Indulge me also to do something that I will ask you, for the sake of God and for the loving sake of His name.

Khane Leah. How can you say that we don't indulge you, madman? As long as you are doing your duties for God's sake, you may get as drunk as a pig. But bring in the Purim bread.

Trytel. [*Runs and sings*]

Neither standing nor flying I go,

Swiftly like an arrow from a bow. [*Exit.*]

Khane Leah. Tell me what's troubling you, my child.

Taybele. Dear mother, when Herr Yaffe comes to give me a lesson, would you invite him to the feast?

Khane Leah. Why do you need that poor German Jew? He will only make fun of us.

Taybele. Dear mother! He is so lonely, such a stranger here. He is always sitting alone by himself in his dark room somewhere at the edge of town. He has no acquaintances and no friends. Let him spend a few hours with us.

[*Trytel enters with a large Purim bread.*]

Trytel. Now this is indeed a Purim bread worthy of its name, fat as a goose and heavy as a question from the Great Rabbi of Prague. [*He pulls out a raisin and eats it.*]

Khane Leah. Stop! Thief! Why are you pulling out the raisins?

Trytel. And suppose there are a few less raisins; that's also not a misfortune. [*The doorbell rings.*]

Trytel. Ah! Who is ringing? Surely that's our timid pauper from the Upper School. It doesn't suit him to go through the kitchen. He needs to ring. A joker from the Upper School.

Taybele. Not from the Upper School—from the Rabbinical Academy. How many times have I already told you? Go and open the door, and quickly.

Trytel. What's the difference? A teacher or a rabbi: may all the unbelievers be struck by lightning. [*Exit.*]

Taybele. Dear mother, don't forget to invite him. I would have asked him myself, but I'm embarrassed. He is so proud in his manner.

Khane Leah. I am only afraid that your father will refuse to read the Megillah. You know how your father is.

[*Enter Trytel and Yaffe*]

Trytel. [*Singing quietly and pointing to Yaffe.*] On the high mountain, on the green grass, stand the Germans with the long whips . . .

[*Yaffe greets the two women.*]

Yaffe. Ah, you are still rejoicing at Haman's downfall. A celebration on his behalf. He soon saw that if he provoked the Jew, he would come to a bad end. And yet in that year he again quarreled with the little Jew. And in today's Purim he is hanged again. The old story lives on with its hamantaschen and groggers. [*He sits.*]

Trytel. May you soon tire of the groggers! Tell me, didn't Ahasuerus deserve that God should give him such a gift as Vashti the rebellious for his queen?

Khane Leah. Herr Yaffe, today you must free Taybele from your usual lesson. We are all Jews here and today is a great holiday.

Yaffe. [He stands up.] Ah. Then good. I'll come tomorrow. I don't want to disturb your great holiday.

Taybele. [Embarrassed] Ah, Herr Yaffe, are you going away so soon?

Khane Leah. Do remain with us. Soon the feast will start. Look at what a beautifully risen Purim bread there is. May no evil eye harm it.

Trytel. Since when do pigs eat Purim bread?

Yaffe. [Laughs] Ah. Thank you. Thank you. I have long been interested not only in the Jewish Purim bread. In fact, I advise every Jew to take less pleasure in the Megillah and to begin to think of something that is new. *[Speaking to himself.]* Megillah and Purim bread; that is the whole of Jewish history. From the Purim bread flows practical life, from the Megillah, the Purim story, fanaticism and delusion. Jews! The more Purim bread, and the less Megillah, the healthier it will be for you.

Trytel. For such advice, may you get a pain in the shoulder.

Yaffe. Adieu. *[He goes to the door.]*

Trytel. Don't trip on the way home.

Taybele. [She follows him to the door, embarrassed.] But Herr Yaffe — if I were to beg you to stay . . . I'm asking you to stay for my sake. I would be honored . . . I would find it very pleasant to see you among all our friends. Stay with us.

Yaffe. [He stands thoughtfully.] I will stay if you, Fraulein, wish it. *[Goes back.]*

Trytel. Well, we have a new guest in town! Blessed is he who comes. The Godless Goy is here!

Khane Leah. What time is it? Ah, we didn't hear the clock strike. Your old father will soon be arriving for the feast. Trytel! Go and call the children to come in quickly to the table. And whoever else is with them, they should all come to the table. But quickly!

Trytel. [Runs and sings]
   Neither standing nor flying I go,
   Swiftly like an arrow from a bow.
   [Exit Trytel]

Khane Leah. [Looking at the table] Everything seems to be as it should be. Taybele — come and see whether we have forgotten anything. We don't want the old man, God forbid, to get angry at the table. Do come here. *[Quietly]* I am so afraid — because you invited that German of yours.

Taybele. Don't worry, mother. I will say that I invited him. But you know that I am his beloved little youngest daughter and he permits me everything.

[Enter: Avrom Harif, his wife, Etele, and their children; Moyshe Hasid, his wife, Gitele, and their children. After them Trytel and several other Jews.]

Khane Leah. Do sit down. Sit down quickly at your places.

Harif. I will sit here, at my father-in-law's right hand.

Moyshe. How is it that you always manage to sit at his right hand? Oh, my aristocrat!

Harif. The reason is because I am the older son-in-law and because, in addition, I am Avrom Harif and not Moyshe Hasid. *[He sits down.]*

Moyshe. It's because you are a Misnagid and every Misnagid is stupid and arrogant. Totally insolent and impertinent. *[He sits down on the other side.]*

Harif. It's because you are a Hasid, a Chabadnik, and every Hasid is a . . . I beg your pardon. I ask your indulgence.

Trytel. There you have it — a most subtle cry of triumph.

Etele. *[To her husband]* Why do you have to bother quarreling with him? Is there really someone there worth quarreling with?

Gitele. *[To her husband]* Why do you have to worry, my little fool? Father doesn't love you any less than the Misnagid, that dope!

Etele. What a wise woman you are! Oh, my "woman of virtue," your Chabadnik should wipe your nose!

Gitele. Tell your Misnagid that he should stuff up your mouth with a rag.

Khane Leah. Have you both started again? Sit down, now, quickly at your places. *[Behind the scenes, one hears someone coughing.]*

Trytel. *[Frightened]* Quiet! Sh! Reb Dovidl is coming.

[Taybele runs to the door. All are still. Reb Dovidl comes in and all stand up.]

Dovidl. Gut Yom Tov! Happy Purim! *[He sits down at the head of the table. Trytel stands near him.]* Sit down, all of you. *[All sit.]*

Gitele's children. *[They rise and speak in unison.]* Grandpa, may you and Grandma live well together over the next year.

Etele's children. *[They rise and speak in unison.]* Grandfather, may you and Grandmother live to 120 years.

Dovidl. Khane Leah, go and take out of the bureau the old gold coins and give each of your children two of the coins. I want the children to have a special souvenir of today. And have them serve the old cherry brandy at the table. For me this Purim is a special Purim because the news that I will be announcing tonight will surprise you all. We'll have a little brandy and something to eat. *[All drink and eat. Khane Leah gives a wine bottle to Trytel, and they both go out.]* Children! Do you still remember the "Shoshanes Yankev" that we sang in earlier years?

All. Yes, dear grandfather. Yes. *[The old man begins to sing. The others join in. Khane Leah comes in and hands out the gold coins to the children. Trytel puts a large bottle of cherry brandy on the table. Taybele hands Yaffe a piece of cake.]*

Trytel. Reb Dovidl, may I also have a little brandy in honor of the holiday?

Dovidl. Yes! You are an honorable Jew, and today you should drink your fill — until you don't know the difference between godless Haman, the Evil One and Mordechai. Ah, I haven't even noticed that we have a guest. Our teacher, Reb Yaffe. Please put on your hat and then I'll drink l'chaim with you.

Yaffe. Drinking l'chaim with you is a pleasure but the hat . . .

Taybele. *[Runs and brings him his hat and says with a pleading voice]* Put it on, I beg of you.

Yaffe. For your sake, putting on the hat is also not hard.

Dovidl. Ah, that's the way! Be a Jew like other Jews. Taybele, my dear child, pour him a glass of brandy. Let's all drink. *[All drink.]* And now look here, my dear daughters, at what a platter of Purim sweets I have prepared for you. You, my eldest daughter, Etele, are a skillful person, a wonderful housewife. You have golden hands. For you I've brought two diamond rings for your fingers.

Etele. *[She takes them. Stands up.]* I thank you, dear father. May you enjoy this year in good health.

Trytel. Oh, this is good; this is fine.
Now hand me a cup and I'll drink some wine. *[Drinks.]*

Dovidl. For you, Gitele, my second daughter — you have brilliant ears that hear what is said and do not forget. Therefore I have brought for you a pair of diamond earrings.

Gitele. I thank you, dear father. May the next year bring you pleasure and happiness.

Dovidl. And for you, Taybele, my dearest youngest daughter. Come here to your father. *[Taybele goes to him; he embraces her and kisses her.]* You, my littlest daughter, have a noble heart — therefore I have bought for you a brooch for you to wear over your heart. Do you see? *[He opens the package. All are amazed.]*

Trytel. Today, just imagine, we all have golden hands, brilliant ears and a diamond heart. What kind of gift of Purim sweets is yet to come? I don't wish to be there.

Dovidl. Taybele, my foolish little child, do you have any idea what this brooch costs? I paid 850 rubles for it. Are you pleased with it, my little Taybele? *[Taybele looks down and remains silent.]* You are silent. It doesn't please you? You are unsatisfied with my gift? Speak. Why are you silent?

Khane Leah. [Frightened] Taybele, take your present and say your thanks.

Dovidl. Silence over there! Silence! You should have taught her when you still had a little sense and she had less. . . . Now it's too late. *[To Taybele]* Go and sit down in your place! *[Taybele takes several steps.]* No. Come here. Here! *[She turns back to him.]* Speak. Why are you silent? Why don't you say why you are you unsatisfied? You don't like the brooch? I will buy you a more expensive one, a more beautiful one.

Taybele. [With a shaking voice] I am entirely satisfied, Papa. I am very thankful to you that you love me, that you think about me, that you want to give me pleasure. But, Papa, I don't love ornaments and jewels. I don't understand why a person needs to adorn herself with glittering bits of glass when nature itself has so richly ornamented and decorated her. I don't understand why we need these expensive baubles. They cost so much money and bring so little pleasure. Dear father, I don't want to anger you, but I am telling the truth. I don't need it and the brooch means nothing to me.

Dovidl. You don't need it? Well then — if one doesn't need it! *[He throws the brooch on the ground. All shake their heads, exclaiming, "How can it be?"]* Go and sit down. *[Reb Dovidl lowers his head and is lost in thought. All remain silent. Trytel hands the brooch to Khane Leah]*

Yaffe. Reb Dovidl, the whole world thinks of you as a wise man. Say it yourself. Isn't your daughter absolutely right? Isn't it absurd the way grown-up and civilized people give away so much money for shiny, childish things that interest no one but children and savages? Ah! How many poor people we could make happy with that money which is squandered on these unworthy stupidities.

Dovidl. Ah! Now I understand where Taybele gets her wisdom. She is quoting her rabbi's Torah. Even in these matters she no longer has her own will.

Yaffe. I swear to you, that I never discussed these matters with her. Therefore, I am all the more happy . . .

Dovidl. [Interrupting] Foolishness. A woman should do as she is told and present herself just like all the other women. They shouldn't be philosophizing. Judaism has been dirtied enough by men's philosophy. Perhaps it suits a philosopher to go about in scuffed and worn-out boots. But a woman should have jewels and beautiful clothes.

Trytel. There you have it. Don't hope and you won't get scalded.

Harif. Our holy sages have said: Woman was created only for her beauty. Woman was created only to bear children. And Rabbi Haia says, woman was created only to wear jewels, but they have more understanding than we men. What do you think, Reb German?

Moyshe. Oh, the rabbi, oh, the students! Woe to the teacher and woe to the pupil. Why did God create a Jewish woman?

Etele. I know that I have never refused jewels and for that reason, thank God, I am well, have dear little children, obey my father, may he remain healthy, and I don't quarrel with my husband. May so much be said for every Jewish daughter.

Gitele. What then? Did God create you to be a Jewish woman? Then don't go crawling into men's philosophy.

Trytel. [He pours himself a glass.] The women should hold their noses if they want to compare themselves to us! *[He drinks.]*

Etele. Excuse me, father. I will allow myself to say that you, may you live long, you yourself are guilty. You have taught us only a little, so we are ordinary persons, like all other women . . .

Trytel. Are women also people? Oy, what a pain in the belly!

Etele. [Continuing] Taybele, however, was taught too much, with teachers and lessons and other useless trifles. Tell me yourself, why do we need all of this?

Dovidl. [Cheerfully] Taybele. Come here to your father. *[She goes to him.]* They are all cows. They all do just what I demand of them. And you have more sense than all of them. You are right. Why do you need adornment when God himself adorned you with beauty, with cleverness, with a clear conscience? Give your old father a kiss. *[They kiss.]*

Trytel. It is not for nothing that the goy, may he suffer for our sins, says — don't claim victory until you've made the jump to the other side.

Dovidl. And you, Reb Yaffe — come here also to me, come nearer and we will drink a brandy. I love a clever and honorable man, even if he is a heretic.

Yaffe. *[He sits down next to Dovidl.]* And I love a clever person even if he is a fanatic.

Dovidl. *[Pours.]* To our health. Drink up everyone and rejoice. I love everybody. Today will be a day for me in which I will not quarrel with anyone. *[They all offer toasts—l'chaim — and drink.]*

Trytel. And me too, Reb Dovidl?

Dovidl. And you too, according to my will — even such a clumsy Golem has earned a drink.

Trytel. If that's the case — then I will also drink brandy.

Dovidl. And how about you Taybele? Take a little glass.

Taybele. I don't want to. I can't drink.

Dovidl. Even if I ask you to?

Taybele. I'm afraid I'll get drunk.

Dovidl. *[Angry]* And if I command you! *[Taybele drinks.]* Ah — my dear little girl. Have you already come to the point where you no longer want to obey your father? As long as I live, you will all do only that which I demand. If I say that it is day, you must all also say that it is day. If I say that it is night, then it must be night. Is that so?

All. Yes, yes.

Etele. How can it be otherwise?

Harif. Of course. How can it be otherwise?

Dovidl. And if I say that is absolutely not Trytel over there but a horse, then you must all agree . . . even Trytel himself. Trytel, tell me, what are you?

Trytel. A horse. I'm a horse, and I love to be a horse! *[All laugh.]*

Dovidl. *[Laughs]* That's the way it should be. . . . Herr Yaffe, perhaps you will sing us something, a little German song, a cheerful tune.

Yaffe. No. I can't sing.

Taybele. Papa, Herr Yaffe sings very beautifully.

Dovidl. Well, ask him, you ask him. He will surely agree if you ask him. The rascal!

Taybele. *[Whispering]* Herr Yaffe, please be so kind. . . . Sing us something. I would be so grateful if you would.

Yaffe. Nu — I will sing you something. But not German. *[He sings. All drink and sing.]*

Dovidl. Nu, my Harif, perhaps you will give us some commentary on the Torah.

Harif. If you desire it, with the greatest pleasure.

Moyshe. And I, dear father-in-law, have prepared on my part a fine piece of Hasidic thought with Kabbalah.

Trytel. Instead of brandy, Torah; Hasidism together with Kabbalah. It would be better if Haman didn't court disaster.

Harif. Who needs your Kabbalah and Hasidism? Kabbilah, Kabbalah, Kabbilah, Kabbalah — like mares neighing.

Moyshe. Is that the way you think it is? Your whole philosophy, the way of the Misnagdim, was thought up by the Vilna goy out of his heretical head, but Hasidism stands since the world was created. God himself is a Hasid!

Yaffe. Just imagine. Natural philosophy doesn't even know that God belongs to the Hasidic party!

Moyshe. Yes!

Trytel. And further it is written, a twisted spirit brings forth lilpul.

Dovidl. Ignoramus! Pilpul — sophistry — is what is written, not lilpul.

Moyshe. Adam, the first man, was already a Hasid as it is written: Adam, the first man, was a great Hasid and as soon as he realized that through him there came death, he sat down and fasted for 130 years, one after the other.

Yaffe. Aha! Yet general histories know nothing of this fact!

Harif. Yes, Adam, the first man, was indeed a Hasid, first of all because he behaved like a Hasid, going about without trousers, and secondly because the Gemara says about him that he was a holy man, a Tsaddik. In reality he was an unclean, uncircumcised man. And he denied God. *[Dovidl laughs.]*

Trytel. Do you understand this? The Gemara goes back and forth on this subject, but it's not for nothing that it's said, there's no particular reason for tailoring at all. Tailoring or Torah study — there's no *practical* reason for either of them.

Dovidl. Ah, Trytel, you are right. There is not only deep wisdom in the Torah, but one can interpret every word into a mountain of meanings, just as the sages have said. And what emerges from the wisdom that you study, Reb Yaffe? That only teaches us to shave our beards and go about without a hat. A great piece of wisdom! Ivan, the peasant, who does not go to the Rabbinical Academy, can do that also. *[All laugh]*

Trytel. There you have it. Triumphant words.

Harif. Eight years of study, and no better than a peasant at the end of it!

Yaffe. Although you are all learned and wise, you don't know who God is — a Hasid or a Misnagid. And I know. He is a Misnagid. That is because Moses asked him to show him his face and he showed him his backside. Only a Misnagid could do that.

Dovidl. [Angry] In my house I don't allow laughing at God. If you think you are philosophizing, while you are really making fun of everything that is sacred, then you are nothing but shoemakers and not philosophers.

Trytel. If you see a shoemaker, tell him I need a patch on my shoes.

Yaffe. You don't permit laughter in your house about God, but you allow laughter about a person. But I don't allow people to laugh at me or to teach me what I should say and what not to say. Good night! *[He goes to the door.]*

Dovidl. Sit down. Sit down. I command you to remain at the table. Sit down now. Here!

Yaffe. You command me! What can command me is only my own mind. If my mind commands me, I can do anything in the world! When my mind commanded me in my twentieth year that I should go away, abandon the Jewish commentaries, the Gemara and the Agadah and other studies and take myself off to other learning, I asked no one for permission. When my mind commanded me to leave the Besmedresh, the House of Study, and go to the Rabbinical Academy, I went eight versts on foot in winter in the cold and frost and I asked no one what I should study or what I should do. If my mind tells me that I must now suffer hunger, want, cold in order later to arrive at a goal, then I will do it. If my mind will tell me to carry a load over mountains from one place to another, then I will accomplish it. But if you ask me to beat someone, I would not do it because my own good sense would not allow it. There is no power that can command me apart from my own reflections and my own thoughts. With the others you can play as with pawns in a chess game, but not with me. *[He goes.]*

Dovidl. Stay here. I'm telling you! Taybele, don't let him go. I don't want him to go away from here feeling offended.

Taybele. [Goes to him.] Herr Yaffe, stay here! I am pleading with you. Do it for my sake — be so kind. It would be so hard for me if you went away now. *[Yaffe turns around and returns to his place. All the others remain silent. Behind the scene one hears noises. Trytel runs in and goes immediately to Reb Dovidl.]*

Trytel. Baruch haba! Blessed be he who comes! The Purim players are here! Shall I let them in?

Dovidl. Call them in! Let them make a celebration!

All the children. [*Happily*] The Purim players! The Purim players!

Trytel. [*At the door*] In with you fellows, you rascals. [*The cast arrives:
  Ahasuerus, dressed as a general; Mordechai, a beard down to the floor,
  Haman, dressed as an officer, Vashti, as a gypsy, Esther, men and women in
  fantastic clothing.*]

Dovidl. Trytel, bring the actors a good glass of brandy and invite them to
  begin their theater. [*They drink.*]

Haman. [*With the melody from the Megillah*]

  Listen and watch,

  Soon will be seen

  Singing and dancing

  And Vashti the Queen!

  [*All sing a lively dance tune and dance*]

Mordechai. And it came to pass in the days of Ahasuerus . . .

Haman. Here where one dare not say,

  "The sun rises: it is day."

Ahasuerus. I am the Emperor,

  Full of passion and strife.

  Bring me my Vashti,

  My queen, my wife!

  I am Ahasuerus,

  I rage and I storm:

  Bring her unveiled,

  As bare as she was born.

  [*All sing, as before.*]

Haman. [*To Vashti*]

  Fly like a bird, Vashti,

  All may yet be well,

  But if you don't look and see,

  You'll be baking bagels in hell.

Vashti. Don't be a horse's ass!

  Dig yourself a grave.

  You'd tell my husband he's a worthless lout,

  If only you were brave. [*Chorus*]

Ahasuerus. As soon as I ask you sweetly to begin

  Give a kick outdoors to Vashti the queen,

  And bring the greenhorn Esther in,

  The loveliest girl I've ever seen.

As for Haman, the Evil One
Quickly, hang him! *[Chorus]*
Mordechai. [Sings using the tune of the Akhdomoth]
Of Haman, the Evil one, listen to my story:
Tarum, tarum, tarum
I'll sing of how he's buried, without any glory:
Tarum, tarum, tarum
Out of him has become
Tarum, tarum, tarum
Earth and ashes, hamantasches,
Tarum, tarum, tarum
And I hope the same for you.
And hear what Vashti does!
"I'll give you a punch on the chin, tarum
Broken bones for the little one,
Missing teeth, tarum, tarum."
That evil one, that very one
Ahasuerus, the fool
And now Tarum, tarum, tarum
Oh, Jews, be happy! Tum, tam,
Be happy, Jews! Bum, bam!
Take things easy! Tram, tram!
Sip from your goblets! Gram, gram!
Just be joyous! Tum, tam!
Here is the king! Bum, bam!
Just get drunk! Tram, tram!
That's the end of it all! Gram, gram!
Everyone. Bravo! Bravo!
Dovidl. [To Yaffe] Now, do you see? Jews can do and understand every-
thing. Do you want a Jewish theater? Why, just take a little Jew and
make yourself a theater.
Yaffe. [Angry] Pfui! A disgrace! Is this what you call Jewish theater? This is
a play for the people? "Gram, strom." All of this doesn't matter to me,
but are these rhymes what you call poetry? If you bleat like a goat, do
you think that is singing? If you jump around like wild horses, do you
think that is dancing? Obscene language and coarseness are what you
consider witty. Is that the kind of wit that makes a people's theater?

And that's what pleases you! You laugh and clap bravo! When the foolish heroes talk like unabashed drunkards in a tavern, you think it beautiful. As if that is not enough, you also allow your children to see and hear such coarseness. It's unbelievable. And you, too, Taybele, I wonder how you can actually look at it, go to it . . . in cold blood.

Haman. Oy, a cholera should come on all critics! May a black year be wished upon them.

Mordechai. The Germans are always cutting us down. An ordinary Jew enjoys all our cleverness enormously, and the Germans turn up their noses.

Taybele. I cannot see this as a "disgrace." But I am ashamed both for the players and for the audience. I am leaving. *[She rises.]*

Dovidl. Where to? Remain seated. If I am sitting and listening, then you all can sit and listen. If I am not ashamed, no one need be ashamed. What is theater and acting? A piece of foolishness. And from foolishness, one can only expect foolishness.

Yaffe. And this is exactly the misfortune: that you Jews think that Purim is the Purim bread, the feast, the Purim play. And all that, you say, is not foolishness. But the theater, the most important art in the world — this, you say, is foolishness.

Trytel. According to these heretics, the greatest art in the world is laughing at God and gobbling pig and pork! A fat pig is not foolishness according to them.

Moyshe. *[Drunk]* Well, we will see what foolishness is according to the Kabbalah. Elul is a fool, Chsul is a fool, Petai is a fool, Shitah is a fool, and . . .

Trytel. And a Golem is even worse than a fool.

Dovidl. Well, let's stop talking about foolishness. I want to tell you all something important today. Trytel! Take the Purim players away to another room and let them be given something to eat and drink.

Trytel. You band of comedians come along. Now is the time for eats! *[All follow him. Trytel yells behind the scene. "You there, Yakhne and Dvosye, prepare the table for the Purim players and give them meat and fish and two flasks of brandy."]*

Dovidl. *[He strokes his beard and remains silent. Everyone looks at him and waits.]* Listen to what I have to say, my children! You see that I have not spent my years in foolishness. I stand now amongst the great men of the city. I have done my duty to God and also to the world and to humanity. Now that I've grown old, I want to devote myself to God. Why need I continue to trouble myself with ordinary affairs? Thank God, I have fine, honorable children to whom I can give my whole business. Children! I have made up my mind to travel to the Land of Israel and there to carry on the remaining days of my life in the study of Torah and prayer.

Khane Leah. And me? Vay iz mir! You've never talked this over with me.

Dovidl. Why do I have to talk it over with you? If I tell you to travel to the Land of Israel, you'll travel! And if I tell you to stay here, you'll stay here! Listen to me, children and my clever sons-in-law. This whole time you have lived with me in peace and in good friendship. And amongst yourselves you have also lived in an easy way.

Trytel. Like seven tomcats in one sack.

Dovidl. I hope that without me you will continue to live in peace.

Harif. God in heaven! Why should we quarrel?

Etele. Imagine quarreling! Gitele and her children are as dear to me as my own life. Have you ever heard us quarreling?

Trytel. They'll scratch one another every day. Like cats.

Dovidl. My whole fortune — houses, stores, and cash — is worth 310,000 rubles.

Harif. [His eyes flash.] Aha! May no evil eye befall you.

Moyshe. 310! What does the Gematria tell us? The letter Shin with the letter Jod equals 310! What does the Kabbalah tell us? In the afterlife, God has created 310 worlds for every Tsaddik or holy man.

Dovidl. All of this, I divide into three equal parts and give to my children by blood.

Khane Leah. Vay iz mir! And what will remain for us?! We also need something to live on.

Dovidl. You old fool! What do you mean — what will we live on? Everything! These are our children and their fortune is ours. We will continue to live as we do. Is there any reason to be concerned about us?

Khane Leah. Yes, yes. They will surely take care of you, God willing. Yes, yes.

Etele. What are you talking about, dear mother? That our father, may he live long, is not right? We are not stones. We are your children, your own flesh and blood.

Khane Leah. Well — we'll see in the end. We will see later who is right. I hope that I am the one who is wrong.

[Trytel sits down at a distance and looks worried.]

Harif. Mother-in-law, may you live long and learn to trust us.

Dovidl. I am not asking anyone here for any advice. I do what I want, by myself. Right after Pesach, I will travel to the Land of Israel with my old wise wife. I don't believe that my own children will be able to forget that they are indebted to their father, that my sons-in-law will forget that their father-in-law is Reb Dovidl Moysheles and that they would cease to honor me, to obey me! To remember me!

Etele. Ai! Let God forget us, if we should forget you.

Harif. You are our glory, our crown, our honor.

Dovidl. I want you to divide everything, and that you should live in peace and carry on the business as formerly. I am not taking Taybele to Eretz Israel and until her wedding, she should be with you and be under the supervision of Harif and live just as she has lived until now, as stated in the document that I will prepare with the notary. There it will be clearly written out what I am leaving each of you. None of you is receiving less than any of the others.

Now, my children, are you satisfied? Don't be afraid to speak freely! I want to hear from you, how you will answer to all this.

Etele. Dear father. We and our children will forever be grateful. We will boast of our pride in our good and clever father. Is it not the greatest good fortune to have a father who is so wise, such a teacher, such a pious and honorable Jew? Certainly for your sake, God will also help us. Allow me, father, to kiss your hand.

Dovidl. *[He kisses her.]* My clever daughter! You are the "woman of virtue" of whom Solomon the King sang in his famous song.

Harif. *[He stands up.]* The Gemara says: The Shechinah rests only on a clever, a strong, rich, and a tall man. Father-in-law, you have all the signs so that certainly the Shechinah rests on everything that you say. To tell the truth, it is the will of God. Therefore we dare not even speak or attempt to explain it. Be sure that whatever you have built up will not go under.

Dovidl. A Harif talks like a Harif.

Gitele. Dear, beloved father, what can I say to you? You are cleverer than we are and understand better than we do what you are doing. I am made so sad because you are leaving us and we remain alone. Don't forget us. We will never forget what you have done for us. I don't remember whether you have ever in my life kissed me. Allow me now to kiss you.

Dovidl. [He kisses her and weeps.] Ah, my little Hasidic woman. My quiet, pious daughter. You don't know me. You don't understand me. You think that because I don't kiss you and embrace you like other fathers that I don't love you. Ah. Foolish children! You are my life, my happiness, my consolation. *[Kisses her.]*

Moyshe. Our sages say the world of the Torah will be fulfilled only through him who creates his own good fortune where before there was nothing. You have now, through your own efforts, made your own good fortune, and as you are leaving us, one can say that you have fulfilled the whole Torah. Happy is the person who can achieve that. And happy are the children who have such a father.

Dovidl. I hear you and I feel that your words come deeply from the heart and they reach deeply into my heart. No one can fool me. I need only to look at a person and I see him through and through. Now, my dear little youngest daughter, my beloved Taybele, what will you tell us? Are you happy with your father? Are you satisfied with the riches that he is leaving to you? There has never yet been such a rich bride in Vilna as my Taybele. And such a dowry will soon get a successful and clever groom. Isn't that so? Ha! Ha! Are you satisfied, happy?

Taybele. [Stands up. Is pale.] I know that you will once again be angry with me. But I cannot say something that is a lie. I must tell the truth. With what should I be satisfied? That you are leaving me? That you have left me under the supervision of Avrom Harif? Papa! I must now tell the truth. I am always thinking that Harif does not say with his lips what is actually in his heart. As for your riches! Why do I need your riches? As yet, I think very little of getting married. And I will consider myself happy if you would permit me to study. . . . I want to go to St. Petersburg together with Herr Yaffe to study medicine.

Dovidl. [Beside himself with rage.] What do I hear? From you, more than from the others, I expected to hear fine words and gratitude. I expected you to gladden my heart with sweet and loving words. And you are not even satisfied! My daughter allows herself to say that one doesn't even need riches. One doesn't need to marry. Imagine! She wants very much to study medicine! My daughter wants to wait, until when?! She will become an old maid with a gray braid and will heal the wretched from leprosy. I see that you have no sense. You babble this foolish stuff that your teacher has taught you. Out! I am warning you. And now — away! Out of my sight, you foolish calf!

Taybele. [She goes to the door. She weeps.] I am speaking to you with the same words that mother used. Papa, may you not have regrets later! *[She leaves. Khane Leah weeps.]*

Yaffe. Reb Dovidl, I do not know if you have heard of the world-famous writer Shakespeare. Among his works is a drama with the title King Lear. The old king, like you, divided his kingdom and also like you sent away the loving daughter who told him the truth. Oh! How dearly he paid for that! Yes, you are a Jewish King Lear! May God protect you from such an end as that to which King Lear came. May you be healthy and happy. *[Exit]*

Trytel. Ah! Vay iz mir. However much I drank, and I have drunk a lot, but never have I lost my head! Reb Dovidl, and what will become of me, the unhappy Trytel? How will I live without you? *[He weeps.]* Dear Master, take me with you to the Land of Israel. And there, let there be . . . with pleasure . . .

Dovidl. [Lost in thought.] What did you think then? That I would leave you here? My very own fool, it's understood that you will travel with me. *[He is lost in thought. Everyone remains quiet.]* Well, why are you sitting with downcast faces? Come, let's drink and be merry. Sing a happy song. *[They begin to sing. Only a few drink.]* Trytel, call in the Purim players. Let them dance, do their tricks, make us happy.

Trytel. [Opens the door.] Hey! Fellows, actors, players, come in. Come here with your theater! *[The Purim players run in, sing a lively tune and dance. Everyone claps.]* Quiet! Master! Dear Reb Dovidl. Allow me also to join in the dance.

Moyshe. [Drunk] My beloved, my righteous, my pious father-in-law, the teacher, the leader, the famous . . . I will also dance.

Dovidl. Dance! Dance children! Be merry and joyful. *[The chorus sings in a lively manner. Trytel and Moyshe Hasid dance.]*

CURTAIN

Act II

[The same room at Reb Dovidl's house. The furniture is differently arranged. To one side a child's cradle.]

Trytel. [Walks around the room carrying a six-month-old child in his arms. He looks very poorly dressed and has grown older looking.] Little mouse! Go to sleep, sweetheart. Sleep. If not I'll give you a slap that would make your teeth fall out — if you had any! In my old age, they've given me a promotion: they've made me a nursemaid. May it not befall other Jews! What a good nursemaid. May so much be said of all women! What if the child falls out of my arms and breaks its back and its hip? What if I give its little cradle too strong a push and turn it over? Or if I were to stumble over the cradle and myself fall on the child. Ouch! And only a short time ago, I was a steward for Reb Dovidl, not much, perhaps, but I was allowed to get from Reb Dovidl good tobacco for my good work. I was allowed to have Haroset for Pesach, greens for Shavuot, willow branches for Hoshanah Rabba at the end of Shavuot, wax candles for Havdalah, a good carp for Shabes. And what was the whole of my work? Sometimes, every two or three months, if I wished to, I polished Reb Dovidl's boots. And now that we've come back from the Land of Israel I have to work like a common house servant. Instead of Haroset, they tell me to clean out the stalls of the cattle. Instead of willow branches I have to carry wood and water into the house. Instead of a carp, they have me escort Harif to the bath. I have to carry the poultry to the slaughterer. I have to carry the loaded basket from the market. And that's only a small part of it, I also have to be a nursemaid to Etele's little one — and for all my hard work, I get nothing but complaints. And as for food, they give me instead a curse. At Reb Dovidl's house, everyone was allowed to eat even beyond his fill, and now everything is locked up. For a piece of bread one has to go and ask the new mistress, Etele. And she answers that a Jew should pray more and eat less. But why should I talk about myself when the old mistress must work like a servant and even Reb Dovidl also suffers from hunger and is ashamed? Ah, Land of Israel! Land of Israel! What a fine wedding feast you gave us! May I fall ill, if I ever say at the end of a Pesach Seder "Next year in Jerusalem!" No! Better to be a slave in Egypt. Ah! Ah! Ah! *[He puts the child in the cradle. Etele and Khane Leah enter.]*

Etele. *[In an apron. With a bunch of keys.]* Trytel! Quickly! Mother will rock the child for a while. You go and carry some wood and water into the kitchen. And you haven't swept up the shop yet, you lazy good-for-nothing!

Trytel. Etele, I would rather prepare something for Reb Dovidl to eat. It is eleven o'clock. He will be home soon from the Besmedresh and will be very hungry.

Etele. Go on! Go on! You think that food is as much in his thoughts as in yours. A coarse young fellow thinks only of gobbling his food and swilling his drink.

Trytel. And even if Reb Dovidl is a scholar, do you think he can live on miracles? On the contrary, my stomach can manage with what there is. But Reb Dovidl really needs to eat. It's been many long years since Trytel, who once belonged to Reb Dovidl, was a hewer of wood and a drawer of water. Ah, Land of Israel, Land of Israel!

Etele. Go on! Go on! Do as you're told. *[Trytel exits. Etele leaves and returns carrying a bundle of clothes.]* Mama, while you are sitting there rocking the cradle, you can sort these clothes and see what needs to be mended. And you can sew on the buttons where they are needed.

Khane Leah. How unhappy this all is! What kind of a seamstress am I with my old eyes?

Etele. But you have eyeglasses. Is sewing on a button such a fine skill? Vay iz mir. According to them every little thing is a big enterprise. I must say I can't understand how people can sit around idle and empty-handed. I think I would go crazy if I didn't have anything to do. *[Exit]*

Khane Leah. *[She rocks the child and sings.]* Oh, oh, little one. Sleep, sleep, little girl. *[The melody grows sadder and sadder; she weeps bitterly and wipes her eyes with her apron. She falls asleep. The orchestra plays a lullaby quietly.]*

Dovidl. *[Enters. Much older and poorly dressed, but clean. He stands and looks down at his old wife and shakes his head.]* Khane Leah, are you sleeping?

Khane Leah. *[She wakes up.]* Oh! It's you. What's new, then? I must have fallen asleep.

Dovidl. And your old eyes are weeping. What a beautiful old age we have lived to experience. Beautiful! *[He walks about.]* My fault! My fault!

Khane Leah. Why do we have to talk about it? It's over and done with. The cleverest person can also do something foolish sometimes.

Dovidl. Over and done with! It's too late, too late for remorse. *[He takes off his kapote and his hat and sits down at a table at the side of the room and begins to read.]*

Khane Leah. But now you certainly want to eat.

Dovidl. Yes! Actually I'm fainting away with hunger. I haven't had anything to put in my mouth today.

Khane Leah. I'll go right now and see if I can get something to eat for you. *[Exit.]*

Dovidl. *[Alone]* My fault! My fault! I was a rich man and made myself a pauper. I was once a clever man and have turned myself into a fool. I was an honorable man and have become a shame to Israel, so that there is not a moment when I am not sinning before God.

Khane Leah. Everything is locked up. Vay iz mir. What shall we do?

Dovidl. Why do you think it's such a misfortune? Don't forget, little fool, the less I eat, the less the worms will have to enjoy after my death. May they have little pleasure from it.

Khane Leah. It would have been better if we had remained in Eretz Israel. Returning here has become a bitter misery.

Dovidl. In Eretz Israel! To be among a bunch of sluggards, hypocrites, and parasites who think very seldom about God and his Torah and are totally occupied with getting charity from coins that have been begged from Jews abroad What did you want? That Dovidl Moysheles should also become a parasite and live from the proceeds of those collectors eternally traveling through Europe begging for charity? No. I had to go home to my thankless children. They haven't gotten rid of me yet. I'm still alive! I'm still alive and in this world. *[Gitele and Trytel come in. Trytel takes Reb Dovidl's bag and hat.]*

Gitele. Father—did you see my Moyshe in the Besmedresh? It's a misfortune, what has been happening to him. Recently he has been getting drunk with his Hasidim every day. Ai! Ai! What an unhappy man! We have all been unhappy, since you left us and gave us over into the hands of that Misnagdish bloodsucker.

Trytel. Ai! He's grown so thin! May Harif's hands and feet and all of him be crippled. Reb Dovidl, have you already had something to eat? Vay iz mir. No one remembers at all that he goes about hungry for days on end. But I don't forget. Because I myself am hungry—like a whole squadron of dogs. Well, I'll go to our "woman of virtue" and see whether I'll be able to coax her to give me something for the master. And because of his merit, I may also enjoy something. *[Exit.]*

Gitele. Father! Taybele has been here twice today. She wants to say a special farewell to you. Tomorrow she is leaving for St. Petersburg. Just like that. Foolishness, foolishness. And she will actually become a doctor and in time she will laugh at all of us.

Dovidl. She is certainly laughing. Laughing even now at all of us. I have already told you several times that you shouldn't tell me about her. I don't want to know about her. I don't want to recognize her. She! She grieves my heart more than anyone. Whatever wrongs Harif may commit, he is still a Jew among us and hasn't left Judaism. She, however, is in my eyes worse than a convert. Don't tell me anything about her! I don't want to hear and don't want to know.

[Enter Trytel]

Trytel. Etele won't give up the keys. She says that you two will eat something hot. And "Don't you see that I don't have any time?"

Gitele. You've left us in good hands! In good hands! We'll have you to thank forever!

Khane Leah. Now be quiet. Why do you have to pour salt into his wounds?

Dovidl. No. No. Don't be silent. Remind me at every moment of what foolishness I engaged in. Draw my blood from me drop by drop. Punish me. And don't show me any mercy. I have earned it all; earned it all. *[He covers his face with both hands and remains still.]*

Trytel. *[Quietly]* Ai! Ai! Do I want to eat! Right away a thousand voices will begin to speak in my belly. *[Etele comes in. She is carrying a radish and a roll.]*

Etele. Father! Would you like to eat something? Begin meanwhile with a bit of radish and a roll. Soon we'll sit down to our midday meal.

Dovidl. I have already had enough, my daughter. I have already had enough. Thank God! *[He pushes the food away from himself.]*

Etele. [To Gitele] And that "woman of virtue" of mine, sits around like a lazy lump. And that husband of yours gets drunk with his Chabadniks whole days at a time. There is no one to rely on from here to there. Yes. Weeping, getting angry, playing around — that's all that you know how to do. After that, you all go about feeling great. And Avrom and I work like donkeys. My Avrom doesn't even have time to sit down.

[Avrom, Taybele, and Yaffe enter. Yaffe sits down tentatively. Taybele remains standing, looking confused.]

Harif. [Just as if he doesn't see anyone. Speaking to Taybele.] Well, well, Taybele. Father-in-law, may he be well, is correct. He says that only a dissolute girl can abandon Judaism for medicine. I won't give you any money, you sly schemer. Despite everything, just like father-in-law, I simply can't do it. Ah! There is father-in-law sitting here, may he be well.

Khane Leah. [Not happy.] Come here, Taybele. How are you?

Dovidl. What's going on? What are you celebrating, you old fool? *[Khane Leah lowers her eyes.]*

Taybele. I'm all ready to go and am leaving today for St. Petersburg.

Etele. Are you really going away? Yes? Then tomorrow after the cold kugel at midday, we'll say goodbye. We've had enough disgrace and shame from you since you went away from us and became a teacher.

Trytel. No! According to you, she should have remained a servant under you and acquired wisdom from your Harif.

Taybele. [She goes to her father.] Papa. Why are you angry with me? Why do you not want to see me and not talk to me? What have I done that's so bad? *[The old man looks down at his book and remains silent. Everyone looks at them.]*

Trytel. Before we go any further, who besides me wants to have something to eat? So that my soul doesn't pass away. *[He steals the radish and the roll.]* As I am a Jew, my soul is already fluttering at the end of my nose. *[He sits down in a corner and eats.]* And this is not the right way as you can see. I'm so hungry that I began to eat even without washing, and without making the blessing over bread. Let my sins, my failings, my errors fall on the Misnagid's head, all my sins and failings.

Taybele. You are not even answering me, papa.

Dovidl. Away from my sight! I don't know you any more.

Taybele. Once you loved me so. How have I sinned against you?

Harif. She even has the impertinence to ask! Now what can you say to such impudence? What shame! What a disgrace!

Dovidl. Yes, I loved you because once you were an honorable child. Today, however, you are dissolute. Once you were a pious child, and today you only want to be with Gentiles and heretics. Once you were a Jewish child, and now you have ideas in your head . . . the devil only knows what. I ordered you to remain with Harif. And when I came back from Eretz Israel, I no longer found you here. You had actually become a teacher. Dovidl Moysheles' daughter — a teacher!

Taybele. Then you don't understand, Papa, how hard it was for me here without you both. I didn't want and couldn't stand to see what was happening in our house. I wanted to study and to work. Dear Father! Don't be angry with me. I don't want to do anything that will hurt anyone. I want to be a useful person.

Dovidl. She wants to be a useful person! Good! Good! Be a useful person. Be what you want! Good heavens! Be what you want! What do you want from me? Free yourself. What do you want me to do? Why do you make me crazy? Why do you enrage me? No one has any pity for me! No one recognizes me any longer for a father. No one asks my wishes. Dovidl Moysheles is no more. Although he's still alive, you've buried him. And you've all become free and easy! Away! Away! Out of my sight.

Taybele. Papa! I don't want to offend you. I don't mean to do you any harm. *[She weeps.]*

Khane Leah. [She also weeps.] Fool that I am, your old and foolish mother, I can feel what a noble and precious heart you have.

Harif. She won't do him any harm, but she creeps into his soul — God knows how. And you, mother-in-law, you are getting mixed up in this. Why are you crying? Do you also want to travel away to study? Or do you wish perhaps to be a doctor? A girl who should already have been married is a teacher! Fine thing! You are now the clever ones! You understand better: how all of that can be useful depends on which people you know. My daughter would never do such a thing — to become a nihilist!

Taybele. Papa. You are a clever man, and you shouldn't be angry until you realize how important it is what I am saying. You see yourself how unhappy I am. I want to be free — to be equal to men. I don't want to be like the drudges who lead useless lives, who are servants or caretakers of their husbands. I want to live like a person and be a useful member of society. Ah! How hard it is for women to tear off the chains that rivet us to the old ways. All are against us. They make a joke out of our most sacred efforts. You think of us as weak creatures. But we will free ourselves.

Moyshe. [*With a coarse bag for his prayer shawl under his arm.*] Ram-ta-ta-tiri, tiri-ram-tereram. Good morning, rabbis and gentlemen. Father-in-law, you have surely forgotten that today is the anniversary of Reb Mendele's death, may his memory be blessed.

Gitele. So soon, you're drunk again. Gevalt! What is it that you have to be drunk about? What will become of us?

Moyshe. I am drunk? You're lying. I am only a little tipsy as an honorable Hasid should be. Why should I stay home? What do I have to do at home? You can bang your head against the wall — and that's all. The Misnagid is the big boss. And I would rather not miss my good times with the Hasidim in the Besmedresh. There's always a little liquor there. Here someone has just finished reading a tractate of the Talmud and there's a celebration. One drinks a little brandy. Here someone is observing an anniversary of a death. One drinks, little by little, some brandy. Holidays seem to happen every day. The rabbi's wife has given birth; someone's grandchild got married; the rabbi's messenger has arrived to collect money from Jews. Or a Chabadnik has quarreled with his old lady — out with the whiskey! With another one, the old lady is going to the Mikvah, let's have a drink of brandy! What then should I do? Sit here and stare the Misnagid in the face! But he shouldn't hear this, that ornament in Israel.

Etele. I hope someone knocks your teeth out. You're not worth the dust on the soles of Harif's shoes.

Moyshe. Etele, why are you cursing? It's not that I have anything against you. On the contrary you please me. You're not such a turkey-hen as my old lady over there. Father-in-law, if only I were in the Misnagid's place, I would tell you openly in the Hasidic style, what you are. You have deserved it that I should rule over you. Earned it soundly! As I am a Jew! But you are an old man, a learned scholar and I don't want to, God forbid, offend you. [*He weeps.*] You yourself apparently behaved like a fool and we are all objects of scorn. A wise man, ha! A wise man!

May all Misnagdim have such a good year. What kind of a wise man are you, that you yourself crept into the Misnagid's paws?

Dovidl. [To Gitele] Take him away from here, your drunk. Take him outside.

Khane Leah. Vay! What has become of our son-in-law?

Gitele. Go to sleep! Go!

Trytel. [He stands up.] Eh! Reb Moyshe Hasid, you are beginning to act like a thug against Reb Dovidl. Away! Go to sleep! Come, come. Sleep. *[He pulls him out. Gitele follows them. Trytel returns immediately. One hears Moyshe Hasid protesting.]*

Dovidl. [He buries himself in a book.] Ai! Ai!

Etele. Why are you so upset, dear father? After all, that's your beloved son-in-law. You thought that he was better than my Avrom Harif. What is my Harif? He is incapable of getting drunk; he would never be impudent. That much I know. But what I cannot understand is why Taybele comes here.

Yaffe. I will tell you why she comes here — because she is not so faithless as you believe. She truly loves her parents. I know how it grieves her, when she sees the situation of her old parents here. I know that she lives only with the hope that very soon she will be able to tear her parents away from here and find the means so that her father and mother will be able to spend their last years in peace and happiness. That's all she speaks of; that's all she thinks of. If the Misnagid does not want to see her, then I understand that he is afraid that she will demand her portion. You, Reb Dovidl, are still playing the role of King Lear and don't want to understand who is your true friend, who really loves you! You also think of it as a crime that she didn't want to be instructed and oppressed by Harif. So she made up her mind to earn her own bit of bread honorably. You should be proud of such a child. Not only you, but the entire Jewish people can be proud of such a noble daughter. Some day you will see that even a woman will settle accounts with Harif.

Trytel. Ah! It's no joke that Taybele appeals to him. As I am a Jew, the heretic also understands business.

Harif. Must I suffer to hear such shameful remarks against you, my sweet father-in-law, and to hear morals from such a debauched fellow?

Yaffe. Reb Harif — hold your tongue!

Harif. Debauched heretic!

Dovidl. Why are you all attacking me? Why are you tormenting me? Leave me in peace! Each of you — go your own way. Do what you want. You are now the wise men. I am not interfering. *[Angrily]* But while I am still alive, I will not live among strangers. I don't want to act, in front of others, as if I have something to be proud of. Get away from me!

Etele. [To Taybele] Go away! Go away from here with your fine fellow. Only when you are here is there this squabbling over a gift.

Trytel. Because of her, there's war over presents? Ai! May your lying little tongue dry up!

Taybele. I came to take a special goodbye. Before going away for a long time, I wanted to reconcile with father.

Dovidl. To reconcile with me! Never. Under no circumstances! Never in the world! Until my death, I will always remember that even my smallest daughter did not do what I wished but acted according to her own will. That I will never forget.

Taybele. Oh! How hard it is to reach our goal. *[To Harif]* Can I ask you to promise me that every month you will send me a small sum? I don't need a lot. I am only asking twenty-five rubles a month. Twenty is also enough.

Harif. I don't have any money for your upkeep.

Etele. There's absolutely nothing! Twenty rubles, just thrown away in the streets! Whoever heard of such a thing?

Taybele. Papa gave me a portion. I don't need the whole of it. But also, if Father has not taken back his word, I have the right to it. Papa! Allow me to take a little money.

Dovidl. Dovidl Moysheles does not take back his promise. He has no regrets and does not go back on his word. That which I have said once is holy forever.

Etele. What do you say to such impudence! She thought that Father, may he be well, can change his word from yes to no! Well, what do you say to her?

Taybele. When I ask you to give me money for my essential needs, I am not asking you for my entire portion.

Harif. She makes demands! And what will you do, my tough hard-worker, if I won't give you a hearing? Now you are demanding a little and what will I do if after that you demand — God only knows — how much? No! One doesn't have to study! I don't want such a sin to be on my head! I won't give any money for this "evil inclination." You will go on, God forbid, to convert, and my soul will be against you in the torments of Hell. May such evils befall my enemies.

Taybele. My God. What does one do? What does one do?

Harif. You want to study medicine and become a Christian woman? It would be worth something to know that you would stop bothering us forever and to know that you will not be causing us any more disgrace and that you will go somewhere far away from us. Sign this agreement at the notary that you give up any claim against us and that you will never demand anything from us. Then I will give you however much you need for your crafty devices.

Dovidl. [He stands up.] Trytel! Bring me my coat and hat. I can't stand to look at this. I can't bear it any longer. [Trytel helps him get dressed.]

Trytel. Ai! What a bent back. May that Misnagid choke!

Yaffe. Taybele! Come! There is nothing more for you to do here. Don't fall into their trap. I didn't have a rich father. I didn't get any help from anyone. But I didn't let that divert me from my path. Hold up your head and look the future right in the eye as I do. There is nothing to be frightened of. Every person, if he wants it, if he has higher strivings, can make do with little. We will both work hard and earn what we need to live. Don't be afraid. You won't die of hunger or want. Give me your hand and both of us together — we'll go on to our goal! Come! We will show them that the light of science cannot be extinguished by the limp hand of a foolish fanatic. [Taybele gives him her hand, and they both go to the door.]

Taybele. [Stops at the door.] Papa! Be well! Dear Mother, I hope that with time you will forgive me and love me as you once did. Precious dear mother, be well. [Both exit.]

Khane Leah. [She waves after her.] Taybele! My dear child. Keep on! Keep on! And weep for us once in a while. [Exit.]

Harif. Mother-in-law with her tears is always making me crazy at home. [To Etele] Tell her that I can't stand it. I hate all these weepy women's prayers.

Trytel. Ai! Avrom, you're a dyed-in-the-wool Misnagid.

Harif. [To Trytel] What are you doing here? Get out of here! He is always hanging around. He can't get over the old-time ways of doing things. I am not Reb Dovidl for you! I'll beat you till your eyes fall out of your head! You coarse lout! You dirty fellow. [Trytel begins to leave.]

Dovidl. Trytel! Remain here! If I am here, you may also be here. That's the way I want it!

Harif. Is that the way you want it? It seems a little thing. But now is the time for you to break yourself of your old tricks.

Etele. Just stop, just stop. You crazy man!

Trytel. [Quietly] So that's also the master of the house! As they say truly, you can't make a shtraymel from a pig's ears.

Harif. What are you mumbling there? I've already told you to get out of here.

Trytel. I only obey my master.

Harif. Who is the master of this house? Who is the master? I am asking you.

Dovidl. Who is the master here? You are asking? I will give you an answer. I have remained silent until now. I have borne everything with patience. I did not interfere. I closed my eyes so that I wouldn't see what was happening here. You thought that I was already no more than a broken shard. You thief, you. That one could walk all over me, spit on me like an old, worthless rag. Hypocrite! Betrayer! You want to know who is here the master of the house? Here, I am the master of the house! I! Reb Dovidl Moysheles. And stand up from your places when I speak to you! *[Harif and Etele stand up.]* I am the master of the household. Hand me the keys, right now, for all the stores, for the chests, and for the safe!

Harif. [Frightened] Father-in-law. I . . . I just wanted . . .

Dovidl. [Stamps with his foot] Silence! I don't want to hear a word! Let's have the keys here, right now! *[Etele hands him a bunch of keys.]* I am the master of this house! And there is no other master here. According to Russian law — whoever has given away property is permitted to take it back from the other person, whenever he wishes. Do you know that?

Harif. That is exactly the misfortune.

Dovidl. That is exactly the misfortune! Ha! Ha! Ha! Don't be frightened. Don't concern yourself. Don't tremble like a dog in cold water. This is not a misfortune yet. *[He stares at him and remains silent.]* Ah! Misfortune — ha! Here! Take it! *[He throws him the keys.]* The Russian laws permit one to have regret. But I will not permit myself to use such a law. Dovidl Moysheles does not take back that which he once gave away as a gift. I hate having regrets and changing my word. My word is dearer than 360,000 rubles! Dearer than Avrom Harif with all his wisdom, learning, and piety! You are the head of the household, Harif. You! Everything belongs to you all! You have the right to drive us from here, to draw our blood, to starve us to death. *[Behind the scene one hears Moyshe Hasid crying: "Let me go! Let me go!"]*

Trytel. As of this moment, Reb Dovidl has not had anything to eat today. He is passing out from hunger.

Harif. And that's why you are angry with us, Father-in-law, because of such foolishness as food. You can see for yourself that I am always full of respect for you. You are a Jewish scholar and you know very well that our sages have said: "One gives food to his father and coarsens his life in this world, and the other grinds him under a millstone and brings him life in the world to come."

Dovidl. [Laughs] Yes, you are very concerned about the ascension of my soul to the next world. I thank you! I thank you! But now you won't be able to fool me. I know already very well what kind of value to put on the world to come. From a hypocrite who spills the blood of others and charms his way to God with sweet talk. Thief! Hypocrite! Betrayer! I have given you control of my whole fortune *[He goes to the door.]* And also you can keep your world to come. I don't need your world to come! I don't need it! *[Moyshe Hasid runs in from the other door, in a talis katan without a coat. After him Gitele.]*

Moyshe. Ah! Ah, there he is the Misnagid! The heretic, the convert, in spite of all that show of piety. Give me my portion! Misnagid and Hasid can never exist together. Oh, to be the master of the house oneself!

Harif. Go! Go, you drunkard! Don't make a commotion! You are not at your rebbe's house celebrating the third Sabbath meal.

Etele. [To Gitele] What have you done to him? *[To Moyshe]* You clumsy Golem. He's going to wake up the baby.

Gitele. You are yourself a clumsy Golem!

Trytel. Kill him! Kill him!

Moyshe. Thief! I will tear out my money from your Misnagdish throat!

Etele. Take him away from here. May he be burnt in a fire!

Gitele. Why are you cursing him? May you be torn into pieces!

Trytel. That's the way! Cut into a saintly man! Cut into him!

Etele. Be quiet, you pumpkin-eater!

Gitele. You shameless swindler!

Trytel. Throw the dice! Throw the dice and start the game over!

Moyshe. I'll teach you a serious lesson from beginning to end. I'll show you who's older!

Harif. I'll soon stuff up your Hasidic nose. I'll teach you respect! And here's one for good measure. *[He moves toward him to strike him.]*

Moyshe. Ai! Just let me catch your little yellow beard, you arrogant know-it-all! *[He grabs for his beard and they wrestle; they hit one another; the women enter the fray, and it becomes a total free-for-all.]*

Trytel. *[He makes a barrier of two benches, hides behind them and cries out]* Help! Murder! Help!

CURTAIN

Act III

[The same room in Reb Dovidl's house. Five years have gone by. The furniture has grown shabby. Trytel is alone. He rocks a child in a cradle and sings.]

Trytel. Ah, ah, ah, dear baby girl,
    I'll tell you a tale, my little honey.
    Nothing sweet lasts forever,
    Not happiness, not money.
    Sleep little girl, sleep, sleep, maidel,
    The world spins like a draydel.

    A little while ago I was a boy,
    And what has become of all my joy?
    Yesterday Trytel was Number One;
    Today he's the butt of jokes and fun.
    Sleep little girl, sleep, sleep, maidel,
    The world spins like a draydel.

    Today a person is rich and strong;
    Tomorrow, like Trytel, it's all gone wrong.
    Yesterday Trytel was a very clever fellow
    Today he's the goat, foolish and yellow.
    Sleep little girl, sleep, sleep, maidel.
    The world spins like a draydel.

    Today a rich man, a wise man, a hero;
    Tomorrow — a pauper, a simpleton, a zero.

Today a magnate, he's everyone's kin;
Tomorrow, convicted of nameless sin.
Sleep little girl, sleep, sleep, maidel,
The world spins like a draydel.

Today sees a pretty little girl's birth;
Tomorrow she's buried deep in the earth
Today a man's healthy, hale, and sound;
Tomorrow, alas, he sleeps underground.
Sleep little girl, sleep, sleep, maidel,
The world spins like a draydel.

Today she kisses me and is so in love;
Tomorrow she's buried deep in her grave.
Yesterday how wise was the little wife;
Today the old cow is full of strife.
Sleep little girl, sleep, sleep, maidel,
The world spins like a draydel.
Ah! Trytel! Trytel! How hard it is for someone who has no money in
his purse.

Taybele. [Enters] Oh, how my heart is beating! I am again in the house
where I grew up and spent my young years. Five years and I haven't
seen anyone. How are my old father and dear mother now? Ah! Look
at how old Trytel has become! Trytel, don't you recognize me?

Trytel. Taybele! Our dearest has come flying in. I didn't even see you. *[He
chokes up with tears.]* Taybele! Taybele!

Taybele. Tell me, tell me, Trytel, how are things here with you all? How is
my old father? Is he still angry with me? How is my dear mother's
health?

Trytel. What should I tell you? As for me, I've become a wreck. I've rocked
away Etele's three children, one after another, in this cradle. As for
food, I eat plagues and curses, and wash them down with worries and
illnesses, and the only respect I get now is at the market. I would have
long ago run away from here to wherever the black pepper grows. But
I couldn't abandon Reb Dovidl. He has grown old and sick. His eyes
are weak. You won't recognize him now, Taybele. Ach! He is practically blind and can hardly get to the Besmedresh by himself.

Taybele. Terrible, terrible. What troubles he's had. And badly aged before his time. . . . Who knew? Perhaps if I had been near them, they

wouldn't have suffered so. I was only thinking of myself. Yes, I've become an independent person. What has happened to my old parents in that time? Trytel — tell me about my dear mother. How is she getting on? How are they now?

Trytel. The old mistress is also much changed — grayer and old. They're both about to return now. She always goes to fetch Reb Dovidl from the Besmedresh. It used to be that every day I would walk him to the Besmedresh and back. But that didn't suit Etele. She says Mother is of no use around the house. She can go walking with father and you, Trytel, are not too ill to do something. She wants me to work like a horse and eat like a little fly! Taybele, I swear to you that my belly is as thin and dried up as the sole of a soldier's boot.

Taybele. [*She is lost in thought*] Five years. Five years have gone by already. How many hard and bitter days we have all lived through.

Trytel. Nu, tell me, Taybele, have you really become a doctor? Actually a doctor with all the particulars?

Taybele. Yes, Trytel, a genuine doctor.

Trytel. Well, and your shoemaker?

Taybele. What are you talking about — a shoemaker?

Trytel. Ah, I don't mean shoemaker. I mean your schoolteacher, the Frenchman, Reb Yaffe from the Upper School?

Taybele. Ah! The shoemaker has also become a genuine doctor — and what a doctor! If he would convert, he would become a professor.

Trytel. A perfresser! And he wasn't persuaded to convert? Who would believe it? He seemed already a gentile! It's something strange. But he is indeed a Jew. A Jewish soul is not made of clay. And you too are a doctor? Actually, a real doctor? Just like a man! Oh my! [*One hears footsteps.*] They're coming. This must surely be Reb Dovidl with the old mistress.

Taybele. Sh! I'll go sit down in a corner, so that they don't notice me.

[*Enter Reb Dovidl and Khane Leah. She is leading him by the hand. He supports himself on a cane. Both are old and poorly dressed. Taybele looks at them pityingly.*]

Dovidl. [He sits down but does not give up his cane.] Khane Leah, I want to eat.

Khane Leah. Ai! What can I do for you? Listen to me, maybe I can beg something from Etele. Ai, may it be as easy for my enemies to live as it is for me to have to beg for food every day from Etele.

[*Exit Khane Leah*]

Dovidl. What are you sighing for, you fool?

Trytel. I am so hungry that my belly is blowing the shofar. Every once in a while a Grand Blast.

Dovidl. Ai, ai.

Trytel. If Taybele had been our mistress, would we have suffered in this way?

Dovidl. Taybele! Why have you suddenly reminded yourself of Taybele?

Trytel. Who is telling you that I reminded myself of Taybele? I have absolutely not reminded myself of Taybele. I was just saying it by chance. And you, have you totally forgotten Taybele?

Dovidl. Forget? You fool! Who can forget that one child? And such a child. There are no other children who are so beloved, so fine, so dear. Ach! Trytel, that was a special child. She I loved with a very special, different kind of love. No matter how stony my heart had been, as soon as I saw her, it became soft. No matter how angry I was, when I just saw her charming smile on her lovely lips, I also used to feel better. No matter how sad I was, as soon as I saw her shining eyes, my heart would feel lighter, so happy. Ah, Trytel, I can tell you I loved that child so much. She was my consolation, my life, my joy. *[He listens. Taybele is weeping.]* Who is here? It seems to me that someone is weeping.

Trytel. No one is weeping. It was just me, blowing my nose. Once again I have, may it not happen to you — a cold. If one eats so little, one takes a chill. Tell me, Reb Dovidl, would you see Taybele, now?

Dovidl. See her! Ah! I will never be able to see anyone anymore. For me, the world has vanished forever. The whole world has sunk away into a dim, dark abyss. *[Taybele weeps.]* I have earned it! I always thought that I was a strong, powerful man, that I had enough strength to shape the whole world according to my desires and now I am weaker than a fly. I used to think that I saw and understood everything better than others. God has shown me that a little dog that's three days old sees more than me, more than Dovidl, the wise man, the rich man, the hero! Yes! I only now see myself, my own unjust world. The outer world, however, has vanished from me, become dark forever, forever!

Taybele. *[She runs to her father.]* No, no. You will yet see! Your Taybele whom you once so dearly loved is now a doctor . . . father! Dear father! *[She falls on his neck.]*

Dovidl. My Taybele! My child! *[He embraces her and quickly lets her go.]* You were here the whole time. You listened in to everything?

Taybele. Yes! Papa! I heard how beloved and dear I was to you once.

Dovidl. Yes, yes. Once, a long time ago. As for that which once was, that has gone and will not return. I once loved you. But now . . . I can't forget how you made a fool of me. You, I expected you to be a quiet and obedient child. I was sure that you would never go against my will, would never take a step in your life without my permission; yet as it turned out, the quiet Taybele was no better than any of them. She can also make her father into a fool. Now what do you want from me?

Taybele. I want to convince you that I never fooled you. I want to convince you that I have always loved you with all my heart. I want you and my dear old mother — I want you both to stop suffering from want and shame. I am no longer a child. I can now protect my parents! *[She opens one of his sick eyes.]* Papa! I am now a doctor. I believe that we will succeed in healing your sick eyes and you will once again be well and happy.

Dovidl. No, Herr Doctor. You won't be able to restore with your women's cleverness, that which God has taken away from me. . . . I thank you! Go and look for a practice somewhere else . . . I don't need it. I am not changing my mind! I don't change my opinion! I don't believe in any sweet words! Let me be. *[He bangs with his cane on the floor.]* You are all untrue to me. You only love yourselves. Get away from me! If I can't believe my pious and honorable children have not left Judaism, should I believe you, a lady philosopher, a nihilist, who is stuffed with worldly wisdom! No! Now it's not easy to fool me. Get away from me! Don't try to affect my tender heart.

Taybele. Ah! Papa! How can I bring back your love for me and your trust in me? *[She weeps. Trytel turns away and weeps.]*

Dovidl. That which is gone will certainly never return. Once I was an honored person and now I am an absolute nothing. I was a rich man. Today I am a poor man. I once had eyes; today I am blind and that will never be reversed. No! No! No!

Taybele. Dear father. Pardon me. Don't despair. You will once again have happy days in your life. I believe.

Dovidl. Don't tell me what you believe! I don't want to hear. I don't want to know.

[Avrom Harif, Etele, and Khane Leah enter, not noticing Taybele.]

Etele. And that's the way it is. Right from the start of the morning, it begins — a catalogue of complaints about food — as if they had just arrived from Hungerland. It seems to me that old people who keep complaining ought to listen to what they're saying and reflect on themselves. *[She sees Taybele.]* Ah! Speak of the devil! How are you?

Harif. A guest in our shtetl. The queen of Sheba has come!

Khane Leah. Taybele! My child! Vay iz mir!

Taybele. My dear mama! *[Each of them weeps and falls on the other's neck.]*

Dovidl. What's going on? Isn't it yet time to eat something? I beg you. Give me something to eat!

Harif. I would not expect that from you, Father-in-law. The Gemara says that the older the man gets, the coarser he grows, and the crazier he gets. But that you, a learned man, should only think in your old age of one thing — eating, eating, eating. That's not nice. Do you think that we also think only of eating?

Trytel. What's not nice about it? I have heard it said: study like a Jew and eat like a Gentile. And that is after all the law in the Torah.

Harif. With your peasant's head, what do you know of what is written in the Gemara?

Trytel. Even if it's not written in the Gemara, it's still a very fine law.

Dovidl. Khane Leah! I want to eat!

Taybele. *[To Etele]* Can it be that you're not giving our father food? Give him something to eat right now! Trytel! Why are you standing there? Go and bring some food!

Trytel. Yes! What can I bring you? Everything is locked up, hidden. You think that if we want to eat, we can demand to be waited on with the blast of a trumpet. May I only know evil days, if this isn't true. If only you understood what's going on: a piece of herring arrives — but with aches and pains.

Taybele. What are you talking about — locked up? Break open all the locks! Tear open the doors. He is not only our father, he is the actual lord and master and giver of all this. Serve him food immediately. Vay! Vay! What an injustice! What cruelty!

Etele. *[Referring to Taybele]* She was the only thing lacking for our entertainment, and now she has also come. Where have you come from to order us around? I don't need you to tell me that we ought to give Father something to eat. But I can't tear myself into pieces. One can wait a bit, if one sees that the other person has no time. I myself have not had anything in my mouth all day, and yet I'm not shouting at anyone because of it.

Trytel. You should shout at your own fat belly and your own greedy mouth. For every bagel that she has gobbled up, may she be hit by one of the plagues of Egypt.

Etele. [To Trytel] You don't have anything else to do? Go bang your head against the wall. Go and help Yakhne pluck the goose. Father, would you like to eat cheese with sour cream? I'll bring it to you right away.

Trytel. May the devil take you! *[Exit.]*

Etele. [Goes to the door and meets Gitele, entering.] Ah! Here is the other lady student. *[Exit.]*

Gitele. [She is wearing dirty clothes.] Who is that? Taybele! Our Taybele!

Taybele. My dear, my beloved sister! How old and changed you are. *[They kiss and talk quietly together.]*

Harif. Father-in-law — what do you have to say about our guest?

Dovidl. I want to eat! Give me something to eat!

Harif. I certainly never expected from you that you would make a whole tararam about food. Apparently it seems that in your old age you're carried away by your ideas.

Dovidl. Ai! My head! My head!

Harif. Then, you no longer believe in God. Why? If you believed in God, you would not be so afraid of hunger. The Gemara says: God knows that a dog has little to eat. Therefore he keeps the food that he gets for three days in his belly. Now, if we see that the Lord of the Universe concerns himself for a dog, then he must certainly concern himself for such an honorable Jew as a Talmud scholar. You could even go for ten days without eating and you wouldn't die of hunger, unless it was decreed from heaven to happen. Why should you be afraid?

Taybele. If I hadn't seen this with my own eyes, I would never have believed it. And these are honorable, god-fearing people. No! Things can't remain this way. Gitele — let's go over there and consider what we have to do.

Gitele. Come, Taybele, come to my house. Come for the time being. You will be able to look at my Mirele. She is not so well. You already know a little about sickness. You can tell me if we need to call a doctor.

Taybele. Why does one have to go call a doctor, if I am also a doctor, dear little fool!

Gitele. What's that? You can actually write a prescription? And you can make house calls just the way it's supposed to be!

Taybele. Everything — the way it's supposed to be.

Khane Leah. Well! My wise scholar! My jewel of a child!

Taybele. [To Dovidl] I'm coming right back. I still have a lot to talk over with you. You will have to hear me out and then you will have to return your trust and your love to me. Dear little Papa. After all, you're such a clever person, don't you understand, don't you hear that all my talk comes from deep in my heart?

Harif. Now one can see right away that you are lying. Why? The Gemara says: Those words that come out of the heart, go into the heart. Father-in-law does not see alas what it is that is lacking in his heart.

Dovidl. Go! Go! Leave me in peace. My sick head! Stop bothering me. Is that still too little for you? Too little.

Taybele. [Wipes her tears.] Look! Falseness, cajolery, flattery — all come to life easily and quickly in a place with people who have no heart. And truth, pure truth and love do not reach you. But however hard it will be, I must turn my father's heart. I must rescue him. . . . Come! Come! *[Exeunt Khane Leah, Taybele, and Gitele.]*

Dovidl. Is anyone here? *[Harif puts a finger on his lips and remains silent.]* I have been left alone! It would be better to be alone in a frightful wilderness, better to find oneself with poisonous snakes, ferocious tigers, hungry wolves rather than live together with these false, pretending, ungrateful, and evil people. There is no truth in the world. Lies! Lies! Lies! There is no love — parents don't love their children and children don't love their parents — each only loves himself . . . himself . . . himself . . . I am happy that I'm blind and that I no longer see the horrid masks of people's faces. I would be happier only if I became deaf and would not have to hear their poisonous voices. A great creation — a person! Ha! Ha! Ha! With a dog, food remains for three days in his stomach. And the human being, the wise man, the philosopher, the hero, the teacher, the fine housekeeper — all want to eat every six hours! Oh my head, my old, sick head.

Harif. [Quietly] The old man is letting himself go too far in philosophical speculation. Remember what I'm saying. In his old age, he will become either a three-story heretic or else he'll go totally crazy. *[The door opens quietly and Moyshe Hasid sticks his head in. Behind him are other people.]*

Moyshe. [He is drunk.] Aha! Here there is only the old man, that ancient nothing, and the Misnagid, that heretic. Fellows, come in! Start showing your strength; let's do everything just as we planned it. *[He comes in, and many Hasidim come in after him and young boys (choristers). One bangs on a pot, another a brass cup, a third picks up spoons and forks, and the others hold up bottles of brandy and glasses. They go about in the room singing a march, banging and drumming.]*

Dovidl. What is all this? What kind of noise and commotion is this? What's happening here with you? Simchat Torah?

Moyshe. Among us, today is an even greater holiday than Simchat Torah. We've received a telegram that they released the Rebbe from prison. I want to have a celebration at home. The time has come to show you all that I am also the master of a house. Fellows, shove the tables together. *[Several shove the tables together. Moyshe Hasid pulls a bottle from the hands of one of them and calls out.]* Reb Moyshe Zerach may he live long! *[He drinks. The others sing a "freylich" (a lively dance tune) and dance.]* Eh! Fellows! Who wants another drink? Help yourselves to the bottles. *[Several drink]* Yes! Hear me out. Have something! Go right now and pull down all the pots from the upper shelves and bring them over here. In that room, all locked up, there's cherry brandy. Break open the locks and bring everything here. Today I am the master of the house. I, Moyshe Hasid. *[Several run out and return with pots and cups.]*

Harif. Why are you doing this? You're crazy! Have you lost your last bit of sense? You immoral Chabadniks: I'll soon give you something that has only happened in your darkest dreams!

Dovidl. Go away from here all of you. Don't make me crazy with your shouting.

Moyshe. You, Father-in-law, should be silent. You've long been crazy. You've been crazy ever since you gave over your business into the Misnagid's hands. Once, I used to honor and respect you. Today you are in my eyes no more than a broken vessel. Fellows, drink up. Today we'll have our reckoning with this Misnagid. *[They all drink.]*

Harif. Get away from here, all of you. This is not a tavern and not a Hasidic Besmedresh. Get out of here!

Moyshe. Aha! He's starting up already. But who has the queen?

A Hasid. *[Bends down and takes out from a lower shelf a folded hand towel]* Here is the queen.

Moyshe. Today the Misnagid is the king. Fellows! Take the king and with the queen make an end to the whipping. Lively now, lively, Tararum.

[All stand up. Some hold Harif. One of them has the "queen" and beats him hard over his back. The others take hands and sing a Hasidic tune and dance. Harif yells. Moyshe Hasid climbs on a bench — singing.]

Dovidl. *[Sits down]* Trytel! Where is Trytel? *[Etele runs in. In one hand she has a plate of sour cream and in the other cheese. One of the Hasidim slaps her on her hands so that both dishes drop to the floor. She remains standing, amazed, frightened. Harif himself is on his back and groans.]*

Etele. Vay! What's all this? I was in the cellar and heard these wild screams. Ai, that's your crazy prank, you verminous Hasid! Drunkard, libertine! I'm going to get a broom. Then I'm going to sweep out all of you together with your queen.

Moyshe. A craziness indeed! Go and tell it to your grandmother! Do you have a grandmother? Today I'm the master of the house!

One Hasid. Fellows! Let's lead her also into the dance. The king's queen also wants to rule.

Second Hasid. What are you talking about? She's a woman. A female being.

First Hasid. What kind of a woman is she? She's a Misnagid woman. I hardly reckon that a woman.

Harif. Go run for the police! Why are you standing about like a Golem? Father-in-law, why are you silent with them?

Etele. Here, I'm bringing right away the supervisor! This is a highway robbery with extortion. *[Exit.]*

Moyshe. Father-in-law, better not get into this. You see, after all, how Hasidism burns in us. We could be rough with you too.

One Hasid. It seems to me that the old man is also a Misnagid. Let's take him into the dance.

[Yaffe comes in. No one notices him.]

Moyshe. Don't bother him. In any case, he already looks like someone who's knocked down. *[He pours himself brandy.]* L'chaim! May the rebbe and all of us Hasidim be well, and may the Misnagdim sink in the scale of merit. L'chaim, old man. You've let the Misnagid own you, body and soul.

Dovidl. Trytel! Where is Trytel! Take me away from here. I can't endure this. I can't endure this.

A Hasid. Come. I'll take you away from here. Give me a hand. *[He takes his hand and leads him to a bench. He falls on the bench. All laugh.]*

A Hasid. Don't fall down, Reb Dovidl. *[All laugh. Khane Leah, Gitele, and Taybele enter.]*

Yaffe. [He runs over and helps the old man stand up] You're laughing, are you! You wild, coarse, brutes! You're laughing?

Harif. [He holds his back and groans.] Ah! Curses on your laughter!

Yaffe. [He seats R Dovidl] How is this? The old man has also become blind! Ah! You vile creatures. You laugh at your old, coarse, revolting jokes. You laugh when you should have been weeping and wailing, when you should have torn your hair from your head. Just take a look at whom you are laughing. Look at his old gray head. Look at his pale, sad face. Look at the great tears that run his sick eyes. Is it at him that you are laughing? Are you making fun, are you laughing at such an unfortunate person? If you treat such a weak, such an innocent old man so roughly and badly, then you are acting like animals. You are pleased because some of you took a blind man and pushed him over. Where are your human feelings? Where is your heart? Where is your intelligence? Evil, coarse, wild people!

[Enter Taybele]

Taybele. Ahh! Father, unhappy father. What a situation you have landed in.

Dovidl. Trytel! Have pity on me, somebody send me Trytel!

A Hasid. Well then, there is the new doctor and the lady doctor. What do you say to their father!

Another Hasid. Well, let's take them into the dance!

Moyshe. Do you know the lot of a Jew until he becomes a doctor? Now I'll tell you: a Jew has an angry God but a doctor has no God.

A Hasid. Well then, let's take the lady doctor.

Gitele. [To her husband] What are you doing, you thug? Good God! How is it that you are not ashamed deep down inside? Vay iz mir. *[She weeps.]*

Moyshe. [Totally drunk] What's that then? What do you expect? The Misnagid is making a wreck of me. There is no money and neither love nor life. The noisy Misnagid has stolen everything. And also . . . *[He weeps]* And what am I? I am somehow nothing, eh? *[He puts his head down on the table.]*

Taybele. Dear father, why don't you want to talk to us? Ah, here is Herr Yaffe. We are your true friends.

A Hasid. A very attractive lady doctor, as I am a Jew. What do you say, eh?

Another Hasid. What are you doing, looking at a woman? Turn your eyes away!

First Hasid. But after all, she's no "woman of virtue." One may look at her, according to the Law.

Yaffe. Fraulein Taybele! Come. Come away from there. These coarse young fellows are still capable of insulting you.

Taybele. I can't abandon Papa! Papa, have pity on me, on my old mama. Hear me out . . .

Dovidl. Has someone sent for Trytel already? I need him very much. Trytel!

A Hasid. I look at the lady doctor and I'm reminded of how King Solomon described a beautiful girl: "Two breasts," he said.

Yaffe. [Leads Taybele away by force.] No! You can't remain here! We'll return later and see the old parents and free them from this prison. I swear by my life that I won't rest until I make an end to this shameful and tragic story. I will concern myself for the old man and take revenge on you all. Ah, you pious little Jews. How low you stand! How coarse and immoral you are. How insolent and unashamed! *[He leads her out.]*

A Hasid. Both of you can ride deep under the earth!

Moyshe. [Sings] To the lord of the Heavens, bam! Father-in-law, Reb Dovidl, l'chaim! May God help you. Next year may you once again be in Jerusalem with your Misnagid in the cave of Machpelah. I love you, but who owes you anything when you are such an old fool. You alone have . . . have made me into a good-for-nothing. *[He weeps.]*

Dovidl. [Bangs with a stick.] Trytel! Trytel! *[Trytel runs in.]*

Trytel. Are you calling me, Reb Dovidl? Here I am. May God be with you! What's the matter?

Dovidl. You are here? Come here; give me your hand. You are my one true friend. Nothing but curses and shame and want here. And that's only the least of it. In this house, they are beginning to beat me. Yes! Trytel! Violence, like an old dog that you think can't bite you.

Trytel. May they not survive such acts! Who would raise his hand against you?

Dovidl. Enough of being a guest at his children's house. Enough! Come, Trytel. Open the door for me and only lead me out to the street. I don't need any more. In the streets, I'll be able to go about freely. To whomever I meet, I'll say: " Good person, give a piece of bread to Reb Dovidl Moysheles." For there will be good people, who in the cold winter nights will let me warm myself. What was it Taybele's teacher once said about me? I am the Jewish King Lear . . . well! I will stretch out my trembling hand and will say: "Give a little kopeck to the Jewish King Lear!" Open the door for me, Trytel. Let me out of here.

Trytel. Do you think that I would let you go alone? Would I leave my old, my weak master alone? Wherever you are, there am I! Whatever will happen to you, that will also happen to me. Except for you, I have no one else in the world. Give me your dear, your noble hand.

Dovidl. Ah! My dear, my earnest, my serious friend! Come! We once knew better days, and today, in our old age, we will both become beggars, porters, spongers! *[They begin to leave.]*

Khane Leah. Dovidl! And with whom do I remain here? In whose care are you leaving me? Take me with you also. If such an old age is already fated, well then, we can all three beg.

Dovidl. You're a fool! You, you go to Taybele. She is an honorable and fine child. I, however, with Trytel, will travel a little through the world, and we'll teach ourselves some sense. In a fortunate hour — Reb Dovidl begins a new life. In a fortunate hour, ha! ha! ha! Respect! Respect! Make way for King Lear! *[He falls fainting onto Trytel's neck, but quickly comes to.]* Quickly, Trytel, quickly: Time doesn't stand still. A vivat for King Lear! A vivat for the new, for the blind King Lear. *[He goes out with Trytel, striking loudly with his stick. All stand greatly amazed.]*

CURTAIN

Act IV

[Scene One: A beautiful room in Yaffe's house. Yaffe and Taybele sit on a loveseat and talk quietly. He often kisses her hands. Khane Leah looks in to see if everything is in place. All are in black festive clothing.]

Khane Leah. Now everything is in its place. The guests may come soon. *[She stands next to Yaffe and Taybele.]* Once again, mazel tov to you, my dear and beloved children. Be happy in your own way. I no longer know, Taybele, what to wish you, since you don't reckon as happiness that which foolish and uneducated women treasure. *[She kisses Taybele.]* Be happy, both of you, as only you understand it.

Taybele. Sit down here next to us, dear mother. *[She moves away from Yaffe.]* Sit down between me and your new son-in-law, the heretic.

Khane Leah. What can I say? I can't understand how, when I actually sit down between you, I feel like the fifth wheel of a wagon. . . . I ought to take a look and see how the weather is outside. Such a terrible snowstorm and also so cold. *[She wants to go.]*

Yaffe. Sit down. Sit down here near us, Mama. *[He stands up and seats her. Taybele embraces her.]*

Taybele. Ah! How happy I would have been, how complete my happiness would be if only he were sitting between us now. He! Our old and unhappy father, that wonderful and unusual man whose character I can appreciate and understand. Where is he now in such a cold and terrible winter night? Where is he wandering around now, that wretched, proud, and poor King Lear? *[She sinks into thought.]* Do you hear how the wind whistles and wails? Ah, how unhappy are the people who don't have a warm place to spend the night.

Khane Leah. *[Weeps]* It's already two years that he's been wandering about and will not return to us. It was not fated for him to have joy from his children.

Yaffe. There's nothing that can be done about someone like that. That sort of person is stronger than granite and iron. People like that always go their own way and do only what they decide to do.

Khane Leah. But did he do the right thing as a man? Now he has missed Taybele's wedding. And what a wedding you would have had, if we were living the way we used to.

Taybele. Ah! Mama! No regrets. I needed no other kind of wedding. The only thing I'm missing now is him. My father! My poor father!

Khane Leah. I can just imagine the kind of wedding we would have had for Taybele! The whole town would have come. It's no small thing — Reb Dovidl Moysheles' youngest daughter getting married. . . . We would certainly have brought in the klezmer band.

Taybele. No, dear mother, I would never have allowed my wedding to become such a circus in town. Only foolish and uneducated people have to express their joy so publicly, beating a drum through the streets. A marriage should be precious and holy, and a wedding should be celebrated quietly. If there are no festive clothes, one can also get married without being fashionable; if there is no private carriage, one rents one and one drives to the synagogue without fanfare or goes on foot or by bicycle without the whole marketplace being stirred up. Just to give the neighbors something to talk about, one throws away one's own, often also a stranger's money only to show off and make a commotion. No — that which is holy and dear is far from foolish pride and false glitter.

Yaffe. You yourself must say it, Mama, isn't your Taybele a clever daughter? Hasn't she earned a kiss — right away.

Khane Leah. You both understand these things better than me. I'm going to go and see if it's still snowing and so cold. *[Exit]*

Yaffe. My good, clever, pious, tender Taybele. *[He embraces her and kisses her.]* Who is the person whose joy is anywhere near as great and fine as mine!

Taybele. Do you think there is no one in the whole wide world who is as happy as you? And me!

Yaffe. You! Ah, my quiet dove. My happiness and my life. *[He embraces her.]* You know, Taybele, when I first started to love you?

Taybele. When?

Yaffe. When I saw you for the first time, I immediately fell in love with you. I was happy when I could be with you as your teacher. And you, Taybele?

Taybele. I didn't know what love was. Only when you used to come it was so delightful for me, and when you were late, I became sad. But when I heard your step my heart would begin to beat so hard. After that, when the others were away in the Holy Land and you were constantly with me, then I already knew that you loved me very much, but you were so bad and didn't want to tell me. You still pretended that I was a stranger to you. Ach! In those times there were many nights when I didn't sleep, and just wept. Bad person! You were such a bad person!

Yaffe. I didn't say that I loved you earlier because you were rich. If you had remained rich, then I would never have told you that I loved you. Neither you, nor anyone else in the world, would have believed that I loved you and not your money. Without you, I couldn't go on living and I would have killed myself, but no one would have known what filled my heart. After you became a poor working girl, poor like me, then I rejoiced. Now she will be mine. But it was still too soon to say that to you. No! I thought it was still too soon to talk of love, too early to kiss one another. We first had to struggle, to work, go along on the road together. And then . . . and then . . . Ah! Taybele. A thousand times, I wanted to fall at your feet and open my heart. But then immediately my mind used to speak reasonably to me: Listen! Now you don't have the right to capture such happiness for yourself. Well, Taybele, how much of this were you aware of? Today you know that I love you. Ah, ah — do you know it?

Taybele. [Laughs] How should I know it?

Yaffe. Ah! My beloved! My dear one! *[They fall on one another's necks.]*
   [Someone knocks]

Taybele. Go see who's there. The guests are coming already.
   [Yaffe exits and returns immediately.]

Yaffe. Taybele! Avrom Harif and Etele have arrived.

Taybele. I can't and I don't want to see them now. *[Exit]*
   [Enter Avrom Harif and Etele.]

Harif. Good evening, Reb Yaffe. Mazel tov to you both. Ah! It's such cold weather outside! Terrible!

Etele. Mazel tov to you both. May God grant you joy.

Harif. Even though you didn't invite us, we have come anyway to give you our mazel tov and a wedding present. *[He takes out a gold watch with a chain.]*

Etele. I said to my Harif: Why do you have to wait for a formal invitation? We are, after all, not strangers. Blood is thicker than water.

Harif. The Gemara says: All those who are learned in Science are as if they had lived in the times of the Temple. . . . The sages understand more than we do, and therefore I've brought my hearty mazel tov and my handsome wedding present!

Yaffe. I accept your mazel tov, but as for your wedding present, I ask you to take it away immediately, if you don't wish to make me angry.

Etele. It's a misfortune to have to deal with today's enlightened ones. If one wants to give them a gift of an expensive watch, they become thoroughly angry. Well, well. In that case, don't take it. As the saying goes, we haven't danced with the bear: things didn't turn out as we expected. Well, and how is Taybele? What is she doing?

Yaffe. Well, well. I understand that you don't mean your mazel tov, but I think that you want to talk with me about something. Just say quickly what you want. I don't have time now—our guests are coming soon.

Etele. God forbid. We don't want to keep you.

Harif. What are we asking for? On the contrary, I've come to ask what are you demanding?

Etele. We are kin. Why do we have to quarrel? Today is for you, and for all of us a precious day. Let's conclude in peace. Heaven forfend! There's not anything left for us to quarrel over.

Yaffe. I personally have no legal claim on you. My Taybele, however, demands everything—building a hospital in town for poor people. And demands of you her hundred thousand rubles. Also she requires that you turn over to Gitele her share. Everything that my dear Taybele requires is her portion and should be for you God's law. I have already told you before, and now I am telling you once again that if you don't agree to my Taybele's wishes, I will demand the money from you in court and in addition I need only say a word to my friend the Procurator and he will see to it that you are both sent to prison for a few years. *[He stands up.]* That's all I have to say in answer to your mazel tov and your wedding present.

Harif. Me! In prison! You won't do that! I don't believe it! All educated people are civil people. And as for all that about the money — I don't know anything about it. For what can you send us to jail?

Yaffe. Because of our old and unhappy father. That's why I can send you to jail.

Etele. My God! But we don't even have a tenth portion of it left. It has all been run into the ground. It would be a great good deed, wouldn't it, if Taybele were to take from her own sister the last little bit and would build — the devil only knows for whom — a hospital. Or what is it that you call it?

Harif. Yes! As I live — let Taybele and Gitele take 20,000 from us and let's have an end to it. Reb Yaffe! In any case you don't get anything out of this. Why should you do us any harm?

Yaffe. [*He pretends to be angry.*] Listen to my last words! I'm giving you three days' time. If I can't compel you with fair words to turn over what Gitele and Taybele demand, everything to the last groschen, then I will ruin you both and see to it that you go to prison! Do you hear me! I'll ruin you both! Now you can go!

Harif. Why should we get angry with one another? Look, why are you angry with us?

Etele. There you have your educated people: they're no better, it seems, than others. Let's go home, Avrom, and there we can consider what we can do. [*They go to the door and meet Moyshe Hasid and Gitele.*]

Moyshe. Ah, the sniveling Misnagid is here!

Harif. Go to hell! [*Exit*]

Gitele. [*to Etele*] Poisonous snake!

Etele. Greasy Hasidic skullcap! [*Exeunt Etele and Harif*]

Moyshe. [*To Yaffe and Taybele*] Mazel tov to you both! Mazel tov! [*Yaffe and he kiss.*] What did those two want here?

Yaffe. They came to wish us good luck. Sit, sit down. Taybele! Mama! Gitele and Reb Moyshe have come. [*Taybele and Khane Leah come in, and they all kiss one another.*]

Yaffe. Sit! Do sit down, my dear guests. Is it very cold outside?

Gitele. Such a wind with all that cold. It's snowing so hard that it cuts like knives. Ah! What have they done — our in-laws?

Yaffe. They are not having a quiet time of it. It's pulling them apart. I promise you that you will get your share down to the last groschen.

Moyshe. I want to tell you that the truly honorable Jew — absolutely it's you.

Taybele. The Gentile! The Heretic!

Moyshe. I have always said that the impure Germans are more honorable than we. May I have such a year as you are a Gentile.

Yaffe. [Laughs] Have you always said that?

Moyshe. Always, as I am a Jew. Why do our sages say: there are those who entirely earn their place in the world to come in one hour? If one misses a prayer session, do you think that the Lord in Heaven becomes unhappy? It's of no consequence! But meanwhile let's have a little whiskey. It is, after all, the greatest celebration in the world.

Khane Leah. Look at that, look at that, Gitele. The Hasid is beginning already to become a heretic.

Moyshe. Eh! What is it that our Trytel used to say? When with a Hasid, one should be a Hasid, and when one is with an aristocrat, one must be an aristocrat. So — now I'm an aristocrat!

Yaffe. Hear me out. Since the guests will all want to drink, you should drink too. But I'll have you break the habit of pouring brandy at random.

Moyshe. One should never pour brandy at random. One should pour it directly into one's mouth. Whom are we waiting for?

Yaffe. Ah! Here come some more guests. *[Noises behind the scene]* Ah here! Ah here. Take off your furs! *[Guests enter and greet one another and make gestures as if they are cold.]*

Taybele. Sit down, my dear guests. Would you like to drink tea?

Khane Leah. Does one even need to ask? I'm on my way to make tea.

Taybele. [Holds her back.] No. Dear mother, I'm not going to let you. I'll go. *[They dispute at the door. All the guests laugh. Both exit.]*

A Guest. Herr Yaffe! Lock the door. Taybele will be out there and we'll sing her a serenade! That's our surprise!

Yaffe. Ah! Sing! Sing! I'll hold the door closed!

[CHORUS]

Taybele. [Behind the door] Let me in! Let me in also!

Yaffe. Should I let her in?

Guests. Yes, yes. Now she can come in. *[Taybele enters.]*

Taybele. Ah, what heavenly singing. I can't understand how that has made me think of my childhood and my dear father. My memories are sweet and sad. Ah! Dear friends — sing once again.

[CHORUS]

Yaffe. Taybele! Why are you so sad?

Taybele. I don't know why my heart is so pained. My dear . . . sing for me now your beloved cavatina.

Yaffe. Ah! Ah! It doesn't seem right for me to be singing today. Today I am like a king and I ought to be sitting and feeling proud.

All. Sing! Sing!

[Yaffe sings. All clap bravos.]

Taybele. Here we are, all sitting in a warm, bright room; we sing and enjoy our time with one another. But where is our old, our sick father now? *[She is lost in thought. Gitele weeps. All remain quiet.]* Ah! Who is that? Someone is knocking on the window!

Yaffe. Calm yourself, Taybele. You're just imagining it. It's just the wind.

Taybele. No! No! I hear someone knocking! And every knock echoes in my heart. *[Everyone listens. Someone is knocking on the window.]*

All. Yes! Yes! Someone is knocking.

Yaffe. It's certainly a poor patient. He's afraid to ring at the front door. I'll go right now and see who is there. *[He goes out. A moment later one hears footsteps in the next room. Yaffe enters.]* Taybele! Gitele! For God's sake, remain calm. Don't be frightened. Be quiet. Sh. Sh. *[The door opens. Trytel leads in Reb Dovidl by the hand. Both old, very poorly dressed, terribly frozen and shivering. All are astonished. Voices are heard]* Ai! Ai!

Taybele. *[Falls into Gitele's arms, distraught.]* Ai! Ai! My heart told me something. *[They can hardly keep back their tears.]*

Dovidl. Trytel! Where have you brought me? I feel that there are a lot of people here. Where are we?

Trytel. We are with good people, Reb Dovidl. Sit down Rest and warm yourself. *[Taybele and Gitele begin weeping loudly.]*

Dovidl. What is happening here? A celebration or, God forbid, a sad occasion? I hear that someone is weeping.

Trytel. No! No! Here there's a celebration. They are weeping for joy.

Dovidl. Weeping for joy! Ah! Those are good and blessed tears. Trytel, don't fool a blind man. Trytel, my heart is heavy and uneasy. Is there truly a celebration here?

Taybele. *[She runs to her father.]* Here is a celebration, dear father! The greatest celebration in the world — a celebration that can only happen to children when their dear, their beloved father returns. Dear father! My dear father! *[She falls on his neck.]*

Gitele. *[She seizes his hands.]* Father! Dear father! *[They both weep.]*

Dovidl. Who is that? Where am I? Trytel — where is it that you have led me astray? I can't understand. My sick head can't take all this in. Ah! My eyes! My eyes!

Taybele. Where are you? You're at my house. Don't you recognize Taybele? The Taybele whom you once loved so much? *[All weep.]*

Dovidl. *[He runs his hand over her face.]* Ha! Taybele! This is my Taybele. Ah! My child! *[He falls forward with his head on her breast and weeps violently.]* Is this possible? Is this possible? Trytel! Where is Trytel? Give me your hand. My strength is leaving me. *[He falls in a faint. Trytel and Yaffe lift him to the sofa.]*

Yaffe. Don't be alarmed. He will soon come to. *[Khane Leah enters. Remains standing, astounded.]*

Khane Leah. Who is it that I'm seeing here? Dear God! Father! *[She runs to him.]* Dovidl, Dovidl!

Dovidl. Khane Leah — my dear old Khane Leah is also here! Whose house is this? Where am I? Is this not a dream? Are they just making fun of an old, blind beggar?

Taybele. *[Tears choke her.]* Making fun? Making fun of you!? Of my dear father, of our beloved and respected father!

Khane Leah. God himself brought you here today. You are in the house of our beloved Taybele and her husband, in the house of Herr Yaffe. And the wedding was just today.

Yaffe. Yes! Father-in-law! You are in our house, in your children's house, your children who never stopped loving and treasuring you. We want you to love us. I want you to love me also, even a little, if only because I am your beloved Taybele's husband.

Taybele. Yes. Love us both. And then we'll all be so happy! Dear father, return your old love to me! Why shouldn't you want to love me?

Trytel. Does Reb Dovidl not want to love you? Ask me and then I'll tell you. I'll tell you. Who was the only one he talked of, in the long winter nights? Your name never left his holy lips.

Dovidl. Be quiet, right away! *[Trytel stops.]* Ach, Taybele, I can't believe, I can't believe that you can now love me. Me! A poor, blind beggar! I don't understand it. I would have never come to you. Trytel made a fool of me! He didn't obey me and brought me here — a place to which I had forbidden him to bring me. Trytel, why have you brought on me such suffering and shame?

Taybele. Ah, father! When will you stop offending us and taking us for mean, low-minded people?

Gitele. Not a moment passed, but Taybele would speak of you.

Dovidl. Taybele! Do you really love me? You're not carrying a grudge deep in your heart?

Taybele. Ah, father! If you were only able to look into my heart.

Dovidl. Do you forgive me? Will you forgive me? Can you forgive me?

Taybele. Can I forgive you? You need to forgive me. I went my way, totally against your wishes. Tell me, father, what should I do, to once again earn your love?

Dovidl. Earn my love? Taybele! My precious child. My beloved Taybele, I never stopped loving you. Even then, when I pushed you away from me, my heart was full of love, and I just waited for the time when my child would return to me, my noble child! And as the world grew dark for me and everything vanished before my eyes, there was only one figure that always stood before me. One figure went with me, consoled me, and called me to itself. That was the figure of my child, of my Taybele. . . . Taybele! Don't drive me away from here! Allow me to die near you! Allow me to hear your sweet little voice. My child. Now I can never bear to part from you.

Taybele. With me, you'll always be my father. We won't part any more, my dear, precious, aging, and good father. *[They kiss one another.]*

Dovidl. God! God! Open my eyes for a moment so that I can take one look at her. One time! Only one time!

Yaffe. *[He examines his eyes.]* Ah! You will still see all of us! He has a hyper-mature cataract that we can easily remove. It's not for nothing that you have two children who are doctors.

Dovidl. Too much, too much happiness. *[He faints. All are frightened.]*

Trytel. Reb Dovidl, don't let yourself go like a woman. If not, if not — then I will also be very frightened.

Dovidl. Ah, my fool! What shall I do if my strength fails me?

Yaffe. We have to take him into another room. Taybele, we have to give them both tea with rum. They are weakened. *[They lead out Dovidl, Trytel, Gitele, and Moyshe Hasid.]*

One Guest. That was an amazing event.

Yaffe. My dear guests! Now our good fortune and happiness is without limits. I'm going to serve some wine right away. Please enjoy your-selves. *[He turns around and brings several bottles. All drink. Trytel enters.]*

Trytel. *[He opens the door.]* Let the door be open. Reb Dovidl wants to hear how the young people are enjoying themselves. Jews! Give me also some liquor. If I hadn't deceived him he would never have come. I'm a good person, no? *[He drinks.]* Oy! Today I will take a drink.

Moyshe. [Runs in.] Father has kissed and embraced me. He wants us to be joyful and happy. Trytel, you will be worse than a Misnagid if you don't drink with me.

Trytel. Ah, what a fool I am that I didn't deceive him sooner. I was simply afraid not to follow Reb Dovidl's wishes. L'Chaim.

A Guest. Dear sir—now we'll sing a Russian folk dance.

Trytel. Hurray, hurray! A kazotze! I and Moyshe Hasid will dance. Come, Hasid! That's all. *[All laugh.]*

A Guest. Yes! *[He goes. They dance. The Company sings. Several others dance.]* *[Scene Two: A room where there is only a bed covered with a white sheet. A little table with medical instruments. Several benches. Yaffe and Taybele put on white aprons. Trytel makes up the bed.]*

Yaffe. Nu, Taybele, is your heart all aflutter?

Taybele. Colleague! Don't forget that you are talking to a doctor.

Yaffe. Ah! Excuse me, Herr Doctor. *[He kisses her hand.]*

Trytel. I would never have thought it of Taybele, that she would be a butcher like other doctors. Her heart doesn't tremble but mine trembles like a dog in cold water. Herr Yaffe, how happy I would be to substitute for him in the operation.

Yaffe. Be calm. He will feel no pain. It's not dangerous. *[He listens. One hears the sound of a choir singing a Mass.]* Singing again! That's what happens when they build a hospital near a Catholic church. It's a nuisance but to the devil with it.

Taybele. That singing isn't bothersome. Just the reverse. For the sick person it is surely pleasant. Ach—what an impression that singing makes now.

Yaffe. Colleague! Please stop dreaming. Everything is ready. Tell them they should bring in the patient. *[Taybele goes out and several minutes later the medical assistants bring Reb Dovidl in. He is wearing white clothes. Yaffe leads him to lie down.]* Be calm, Papa! You will make it through this.

Taybele. It's just a trifle, believe us, my dear little father.

Dovidl. My beloved children. I am calm and happy. I believe you, I believe that you will make me well. On the contrary, I beg you to be calm. Prove yourselves. . . . However it comes out—in any case, I am blind.

Taybele. Ah! My clever papa! *[She kisses him.]*

Yaffe. Colleague! Don't forget that you're a doctor! Hand me the chloroform. *[He chloroforms him. The assistants hold him. Trytel stands by, frightened.]* Hand me the instruments.

Trytel. [Frightened] I beg you, don't cut into him!

Yaffe. [Angry] Take him away from here. Immediately!

Trytel. I'll be quiet, I'll be quiet, Reb Yaffe. Silent as a stone.

[Yaffe and Taybele do the operation. Reb Dovidl groans softly. It takes several minutes. All are silent. (Translator's note: The singing of a Mass is heard throughout.)]

Yaffe. Finished, successfully. Cover the windows immediately. But let in some fresh air. *[Reb Dovidl wakes up.]* Nu, Papa, how do you feel?

Dovidl. I don't feel bad. But my head hurts a little. Ai! *[He covers his eyes with both hands.]* A beam of sunshine hit my eyes. The world is once again open to me! The darkness will vanish. How dear, how sweet is the brightness of the light. *[He covers his eyes.]* Taybele. I have Taybele once again. *[Taybele kneels down and kisses his hand.]* Trytel! Where is Trytel?

Trytel. [He goes to the bed.] Here I am! *[He begins to sob.]*

Dovidl. Why are you crying, my fool?

Trytel. Who? I'm crying? May I know as little of evil as my crying. What's all this about crying, suddenly?

Dovidl. Give me your hand. My brother, my friend! Do you see what a fool I was? Always worried, always worried. I used to think that except for you I had no friend in the world. Ah, my children, beloved children! How happy I am. I see once again the wide world. I have seen not only the light of the bright sun but also the light of truth! Today I see that the person who thinks only of himself, who thinks that the whole world exists only for him alone is blind, as blind as I was not long ago. I was against Science! But look what a wonder science has performed. I thought that a woman had to be dependant on her husband. But look at what a useful person my Taybele is. *[Thoughtful pause.]* A person can never judge his own good fortune. Only when he loses everything with which God blessed him and then finds it again — only then can he judge, can he understand his good fortune. Light! Light! The shining rays of light! Science! True and pure love. Yes! Yes! I believe now that there is pure, holy, true love. *[He remains without strength.]*

Yaffe. Calm yourself! Enough! Enough talking!

Dovidl. Ah, my dear child. *[He embraces Yaffe, Taybele, and weeps.]*

[Gitele rushes in.]

Gitele. What's the news? How is dear father?

Taybele. Sh, sh! The operation went successfully.

Gitele. Ah! Thank God! Listen to my news. Harif has just been at my house. He is giving us all our money . . . thank God! Our troubles are at an end! Dear father, dear father. *[She kisses his hand.]*

Trytel. Ai! I shouldn't be embarrassed before the doctor.

> *[Translator's note: The MS ends here; continuation drawn from performance texts]*

Taybele. Dear Trytel, how happy we'll be now that we're together again.

> *[Enter Moyshe and Khane Leah]*

Moyshe. Here we are! I have brought Khane Leah to see how our dear father is. *[Khane Leah goes over to R. Dovidl's bed: they embrace tenderly, and she sits down by him with Gitele, shielding his bed from the door. Yaffe joins them, bending over R. Dovidl's bed with his back to the door.]*

> *[Enter Avrom Harif and Etele]*

Etele. Good heavens! Where has Herr Yaffe vanished to? *[To the company]* Where is Herr Yaffe?

> *[Yaffe turns towards her.]*

Yaffe. Here I am.

Etele. Good, sweet, precious, dear Herr Yaffe! Save us! I won't be able to bear this. We are so unhappy!

Trytel. She talks like a Jewish fishwife and deals out blows like a peasant.

Yaffe. Tell me what you want.

Etele. Herr Yaffe, there are bailiffs in our house! Bailiffs taking an inventory; they are going to sell everything we own! I'll hang myself! I'll drown myself! I'll take poison!

Harif. We'll be arrested, just as you said!

Yaffe. Why are you carrying on? You are being treated exactly as you treated others.

Trytel. Just as it is written in the holy commentaries: as you have put out the eye of your neighbors, so your own eye will be put out.

Yaffe. Instead of all this, it would be better if you looked to see who is here and reminded yourself of what you have done. *[Gitele, Khane Leah, and Taybele rise, and R. Dovidl is revealed lying in bed.]*

Etele. Dear father . . . *[Etele falls on her knees weeping.]* Allow me to ask forgiveness at your feet.

Harif. Forgive us, Father-in-law. Is it not written, "If a wicked man abandons his wickedness and repents, do not despise him"?

Etele. Dear father, we are ready to give Taybele her 100,000 rubles. Tell Herr Yaffe that we will do your will.

Dovidl. Reb Yaffe, what are your intentions?

Yaffe. Dearest Taybele, what is it that you wish me to do?

Taybele. I don't want anyone to suffer. All I want is to be able to open my hospital.

Yaffe. In that case, I will send a message to the Procurator to stop all legal action against you. All will be well.

Trytel. In that case, we'll soon start to eat again!

Dovidl. Learn from this. Take an example from Taybele. No matter how unjustly I behaved to her, she nonetheless forgave me for everything. Forgive one another, children, live in peace.

Yaffe. I, Yaffe, the unbeliever, will offer the first example. Here is my hand. All is forgiven!

Gitele. Come, my sisters, let us kiss one another. *[The sisters embrace.]*

Dovidl. May you live happily and may harmony and peace prevail among you. And say all, Amen.

All. Amen.

CURTAIN

Essays

Why Do We Smile?

Whenever I tell someone of the existence of a version of *King Lear* in Yiddish I am greeted with an involuntary but broad smile. And why not? What two plays could stand in greater contrast? On the one hand, one of the supreme examples of English literature by its greatest playwright, a work at once philosophical, poetic, and profound, exploring the great themes of human life: power, age, and the relations between parents and children.

And on the other hand, *King Lear* in Yiddish? In a language that even its own speakers used to call a jargon? Even if now, with modern linguistic correctness, we do call it a language, yet how do we think of it? Somehow as not quite developed, as suitable for the kitchen, and in America used primarily for telling jokes whose punch lines reveal all the wry bitterness, the double-sidedness of Jewish life in the Diaspora; often, as native speakers are eager to tell you, quite untranslatable. And it was not only the punch lines of jokes that were untranslatable; turns of speech, even single words, as the children of the immigrants soon learned, seemed to have no single or simple English equivalent, but could only be gotten at by long anecdotal explanations and analogies.

Perhaps, I would like to suggest, the untranslatability lay more with the capacity of the speakers than with the difficulty of the language. Although this fact was evident to the children of the immigrants, it has been romanticized into something more mysterious as the language has grown more distant, and the third and fourth generations search for acceptable answers to their loss.

Yet Yiddish is no more translatable or untranslatable than other languages, as its many dictionaries show. But when we are talking about fine
nuances, we are talking about different levels of usage. A scientific paper in
German, for example, translates clearly into English without any loss of
meaning. But conveying a conversation with a Berlin taxi driver would be
a far more complicated enterprise in the attempt to convey unspoken
references and the meanings hidden even in inflections of speech. Similarly, Yiddish on the folk level is a language embedded in a complex culture and would need some unraveling and interpretation to transmit it
accurately.

These were the facts of life that faced the first generation born in this
country—first, their parents' lack of English vocabulary with which to
translate even ordinary words, and secondarily the change in context that
made a phrase in Yiddish unintelligible in English because it came out of
another world. Here is a simple example. "He was so poor," an immigrant
might say, "that he couldn't afford the water for his kasha." We need to
know two things to appreciate this sentence: first, that kasha, or buck-
wheat groats, was the cheap and basic staple food in the diet of the poor.
Even more important was the fact that water had to be bought from the
water carrier. A double expense to cook one dish, but to be unable to buy
even the water was a vivid description of rock-bottom poverty. We need to
know, therefore, who these native speakers in the United States were who
caused so much frustration and are now thought of as the last keepers of a
great treasure.

These Yiddish-speaking immigrants were part of one of the extraordinary migrations of modern times, when one-third of the Jews of eastern
Europe, some two and a half million people, left home for the United
States. Beginning with the pogroms in Russia in 1881, the movement
continued until it was all but stopped by restrictive legislation in 1924.
Those who came were the poor, the young, the uneducated, and they left
their native land and family because of the hopelessness of their lives
where they had been.

We now admire the richness of the life and language they developed in
the enclosed Jewish communities in eastern Europe. But we have to look
closely at what happened to the carriers of this culture in the United
States. Their rudimentary education in Europe, the education of the poor,
was supplemented by a fragmentary exposure to learning in this country
—mostly in evening classes in English for immigrants. Whereas their

Yiddish vocabulary was colorful in turns of phrase, in references embedded in the culture, English was only a poor workaday tool. Is it any wonder that these two languages didn't match and that the immigrants had difficulty finding a translation in their stunted English for a word which was rich in meaning in their familiar Yiddish? These were two unlike cultures, with different vocabularies for their different ways of life. How could the immigrant from the shtetl know the English word for water-carrier, a part of daily life at home, when she had never even seen one on the streets of New York? And conversely the Yiddish terms needed to describe the game of baseball could be put together only with ludicrous approximations. How could someone skilled in turning flax into fine linen in Galicia hope to find the words for all the old processes and tools in a night-school English class? Of course Yiddish was untranslatable for people who had two such different levels of mastery of the two languages. But there was at least one kind of solution to these differences: the incorporation of English words into Yiddish. When Sholem Aleichem came to this country in 1914, this invasion of Yiddish by English words was one of the first things that caught his attention, and he gives it an ironic exposition in his "Motl Pesi" stories—wherein the world is seen through the eyes of a fourteen-year-old boy. There Sholem Aleichem gives vent to his feelings through Motl Pesi as the boy describes his aunt's indignation at the substitution of English words for perfectly ordinary Yiddish ones—"vinde" (window) for "fenster," for example.

But from its origins Yiddish was, like most languages, a hybrid. Although it has a long and noble history, tracing its origins to about 1000 C.E. on the Rhine, the language was never treated with much respect, even by those who spoke it. What did get respect was the Holy Tongue—the Lashon Kodesh, or Hebrew: the language of Scripture, of the commentaries, and of all the learned works on questions of law and philosophical speculation. From its birth, then, Yiddish was marked as the lesser of the two languages, colloquial and homely, yet rich in its reach of allusion.

Hebrew, however, was the province of the very few who had studied intensively and had been supported in their long, arduous education—not the lot of the ordinary poor boy. Most Jewish men read Hebrew because they needed to know how to say the many blessings that accompanied every action during the day. They also needed to read the prayer book during services in the synagogue. Many of the poor who had been forced to leave school early in order to earn their bread could read their prayer books but without understanding the text, and only by dint of much repetition learned the general meaning of the prayers they so faithfully said.

Yiddish came into being at about the same time that vernacular French and Italian were emerging from the general soup of Latin. Yiddish, however, was built on a Germanic base, with a largely German vocabulary. While the German element reflected its point of origin, built into the language as well were elements of French, Hebrew, and even Latin. As fundamental a Yiddish word as "bentshen" (to bless), for example, derives from the Latin "bendicere" with the same meaning. Despite its German structure and basic vocabulary, Yiddish has always been written in Hebrew characters, marking it instantly as one of the special languages of the Jews. Although the lesser of the two, Yiddish even in its earliest days reflected the interest of people in the workaday world, while Hebrew remained stubbornly arcane, the province of the learned few.

The works that were first widely circulated in writing in Yiddish were translations of the knightly romances, then wildly popular in Europe, which were told and retold when they could not be read. The stories of King Arthur's Court, stripped of its Christian symbolism, had a long life in Yiddish literature, with many variations in characters, place, and time, well into the nineteenth century. One of the more extreme retellings has Arthur as a Chinese prince searching for his long-lost parents.

The "Bobe mayse," which is generally mistranslated as the "grandmother's tale," is actually a long-forgotten corruption of the romance of the Knight of Beauvais, which came into Yiddish via its Italian version, wherein the knight is called Bobo. These romances, which were widely known across Europe, enjoyed by men and women alike, had a peculiar fate when they were translated into Yiddish. Then they were regarded as women's literature or were perhaps read by men who were not sufficiently educated to read the more elevated Hebrew writings. The introductions to these stories make it very clear who the expected readers are, and in view of the nature of Jewish education, it is no wonder that women should have seized on this literature as their own. Seemingly forever, whether by law or custom, women had been prohibited from studying Scripture and the commentaries. Girls were taught the necessary blessings: over the Sabbath candles, over food and drink, when rising in the morning and going to bed at night. But all this they learned by rote, hardly understanding what they were saying. Yiddish, however, was the homely language of everyday speech, and everything written in it became their domain, including special prayers written by women and addressing the particular crises in the cycle of a woman's life relating to fertility, to childbearing, to health, to the well-being of the family.

Eventually an ingenious solution to the reading of Scripture was introduced with the publication in the sixteenth century of the *Tseneh Ure'enah* —a series of parables and homilies that closely followed the Scriptural narrative and was meant to be read in its place. Although women heard the portion of the Torah read aloud in the synagogue each week, in the course of its annual cycle, the Hebrew words meant as little to them as the words of the Latin service meant to their Christian neighbors. As one nun is reported to have said devoutly, "It doesn't matter if we understand it, as long as God understands it." Compared to the Christian world, wherein only the educated few understood the Latin services, the Jewish world was remarkably literate, and women especially so.

But Yiddish didn't remain in its birthplace on the Rhine. When the Black Death devastated Europe in 1348–49 this mysterious and unstoppable illness was blamed on the Jews, who were accused of causing the calamity by poisoning the wells. Many communities of Jews in Germany were expelled from their homes. Others were not so lucky and were summarily killed for their "crime." The famous Nuremberg Chronicle has a vivid woodcut showing the Jews of the town of Deggendorf being burned alive in the marketplace.

In the aftermath of the Black Death large numbers of Jews accepted the invitations of Polish landholders to emigrate to their domains, and some ten to fifteen thousand moved east, taking their language with them. There, the ever-impressionable Yiddish, accurately reflecting the everyday life of its speakers, added a new Slavic element to its vocabulary, bringing in yet another layer of complexity to the language. And as Jews spread out from Lithuania to Poland to Ukraine and were eventually incorporated into Russia, not only the structure but even the pronunciation and inflection of the language began to change from region to region: the myriad dialects that emerged gave rise to the mutual sense of amusement and superiority with which each group of speakers regarded the others. What could be funnier (to a Litvak) than the odd inflection of Galitzianer Yiddish? And what could be more absurd (to a Galitzianer) than the way the Litvaks pronounced the "s"? An infinitely durable entertainment all around.

But the growth of Yiddish into a full-fledged literature representing its culture and its people came very late, and it owed its development to the liberating effect of the Enlightenment, wherein what was human was valued not according to class or tradition, but for its own sake. When the Jewish Enlightenment, the *Haskalah,* came to eastern Europe, it brought with it many fundamental changes, primarily in the attempt of its adherents, the *Maskilim,* to secularize Jewish life and in their use of Yiddish as the instrument in spreading their ideas. The daily language of the people moved from its second-class status to a recognition of its indispensable usefulness in reaching the mass of ordinary Jews. "The purest Yiddish is that spoken by the fishwife in the market at Minsk," said J. B. S. Hardman, a Russian-born immigrant who became the editor of the newspaper of the Amalgamated Clothing Workers Union. The old snobbery, based on the distinctions of wealth or learning or the pride in an illustrious family, was being replaced by a new appreciation for the power and color of ordinary speech and for the charms of folk narrative. Sholem Aleichem used the convention of seemingly setting down the unvarnished narrations of a man of the people, errors and all. In his masterpiece, the stories of Tevye the Dairyman, begun in 1894, Sholem Aleichem pretends to be the listener who is simply transcribing the long accounts of events and the philosophical ruminations of Tevye, including Tevye's mistakes and malapropisms as he endlessly misquotes bits of Scripture to ornament a point. Similarly, I. L. Peretz began by writing in Hebrew and then transferred his allegiance to Yiddish in 1891 as he realized that that was where his audience was.

By the mid–nineteenth century Yiddish had come out of purdah. As secularism grew, Yiddish became the vehicle of expression for all the concerns of the Jewish world — not just for women's stories and prayers. Political movements, trade union concerns, new social ideologies such as Bundism, socialism, and Zionism, all found their natural expression in Yiddish. Although Zionists had strong feelings about Hebrew as the national language, they could reach their east European audience only by talking in Yiddish. Gradually Yiddish literature developed in all its branches — fiction, poetry, drama. And as part of its new openness to the world, it quickly adapted itself to the new literary movements of Europe. It achieved the ultimate recognition in 1978 when the Nobel Prize for literature was awarded to Isaac Bashevis Singer.

Jacob Gordin began his playwriting career at just this golden moment in Yiddish literature — at the turn of the last century — and the dialogue in his plays expresses the richness of the language. On the one hand, his characters speak with all the allusiveness that shows a writer embedded in his culture, and at the same time he can write a modern feminist tirade, as in *The Wild Man,* which could serve as a perfect epilogue to Ibsen's *A Doll's House.* In *God, Man, and Devil,* Gordin's adaptation of Goethe's *Faust,* he has the Devil push the Faust figure, Hershel Dubrovner, into an exquisite dilemma that turns on Hershel's conflict with a Jewish law that was a well-known problem in the everyday life of his audience.

Although Yiddish literature was part of an essentially secular movement, it was also exploring the traditional Jewish world and took some of its drama from the collision between the two. The stories of Isaac Bashevis Singer, for example, demonstrate both his immersion in that world and his distance from it. This double vision permitted him to write without boundaries and earned him his Nobel Prize.

The first center of Jewish settlement in New York was the lower East Side, and, depending on when the description was written, the observers were either appalled or lyrical. The earliest writers could not help noticing the evident poverty of the shoppers, the unsanitary conditions of the markets, the dirt and stench in the streets. Other writers were captivated by the color, the liveliness of the crowds, the interesting foods offered for sale, the characters who peopled the streets, creating a cheerful bedlam, with Yiddish, of course, its lingua franca. But by 1910 the vigor of this rich immigrant culture was beginning to attenuate. The theaters, the cultural institutions, the newspapers all began to disperse or fade, and the language with it.

The use of Yiddish declined, in large part because of the immigrants' belief in the infinite goodness and possibility of America. In Russia the Jews had kept a gulf between themselves and the world around them — its language, its customs, its dress, its culture, whether high or low. In the Old World, every move toward the acceptance or incorporation of the Russian way of life was seen as nothing less than the first step toward apostasy. But in America no tsar was forcing his Jews into the Russian Orthodox Church. In America it was safe to become an American. Once in their new home, the immigrants could hardly wait to show off their English-speaking children and applauded every step they made toward immersing themselves in the life and culture of the New Land. Nor did they themselves hang back; they filled the free night-school classes in

English, which they attended often after ten or twelve hours of work. In 1906, one hundred thousand newcomers attended these classes. The majority were Jewish immigrants, and nearly 40 percent were women.[1] These were the new independent women, no longer willing to accept the illiteracy that was so common in the Old Country.

With even a university education available cost-free at some municipal colleges, to those who passed an examination, it is no wonder that Jewish parents felt they had indeed come into the Promised Land. In fact, by 1917, some 78 percent of the students at City College in New York and 38 percent at Hunter College for Women were Jews.[2] It hardly mattered to the poor ghetto Jews that they were unwelcome at the Ivy League colleges. Their free education was enough to move them out of the proletariat into the middle class.

Furthermore, young Jews could go to the university and enter the professions without renouncing their religion, as had been the requirement in Russia. In fact, between 1897 and 1907 the number of Jewish doctors in Manhattan more than doubled from 450 to 1,000, and dentists increased from 59 to 350. By 1901 there were 140 Jews on the police force in New York — an astounding statistic to people from the Old Country, for whom every policeman was a hostile agent of the tsarist government.[3] Above all, the American civil service, with its absolute reliance on test scores and its obliviousness to race, religion, or ethnicity, provided a steady opportunity for advancement into the middle class. Is it any wonder parents were eager to see their children enter public school, where they could begin to partake of the benefits of the Golden Land?

These miracles and wonders came at an unanticipated cost, one not particular to Jewish immigrants. As the children came into the orbit of the English-speaking world, they almost universally abandoned the language of their homeland, which meant that among young Jews Yiddish began to disappear. Even at home conversations became bilingual, the parents speaking in Yiddish and the children replying in English. By 1910 the migration from the lower East Side in search of better housing also broke up the dense Yiddish-speaking world of first settlement. Jews moved first to Harlem and then on to the Bronx and Brooklyn. But these were younger, looser neighborhoods. The new young families of second-generation Jews spoke English, the children spoke English, and even the immigrant generation began to find new alternative English forms of amusement as the great movie palaces of the 1920s offered irresistible entertainment in English.

Yiddish today exists on a number of incompatible levels. It remains a spoken language among enclaves of extremely pious and self-segregating Jews known as Haredim, whose literature is restricted to hortatory children's books, young adult literature, and harmless mystery stories. Haredim also produce transcriptions of sermons by revered rabbinical leaders on religious texts that are filled with so many Hebrew quotations that unless the listener is familiar with these references already, the sermons are quite incomprehensible. As literature, these works might best be compared to that produced by fundamentalist Christians: although the "Left Behind" series, for example, has sold millions of copies, it makes no claim to any literary merit. Similarly the "secular" publications of the Haredim are hardly literature, but rather the sort of controlled writing that one knows from totalitarian societies. The spoken language also reflects the poverty of experience with secular life except on the most instrumental level. Unlike the Yiddish of the fishwife of Minsk, it is without a rich, worldly, or allusive context. What allusions there are refer to the tight religious world in which the Haredim live, but the secular classics of Yiddish literature are banned. In an article published in the *Forverts,* New York's last remaining Yiddish newspaper, in March 2003 proclaiming that "Yiddish lives!" the author makes the point that in some Orthodox communities Yiddish is spoken by young children — surely a guarantee of a language with a future. But as we have seen, it is a sadly impoverished language, one that lacks the resonance of its life a century ago. This is a Yiddish meant for carrying on the prosaic chores of daily life and is filled with English words and Hebrew formulas. One small example gives something of the change in flavor from the old, traditional, pre–World War II Yiddish. In earlier times, when asked about his health or his family or his financial situation, a pious person would respond, "Gott tsu dankn" (thanks to God), which were Yiddish words drawn from their original German base, indicating that all was well. The Haredim responding to the same question say, "Baruch haShem (Blessed be the Name)," an entirely Hebrew formula. In this controlled, formulaic language there is not going to be the freewheeling inventiveness one expects from fiction, while the narrow range of acceptable behavior imposes a firm constraining hand on character development and plot. As in Communist Realist prose of the past, only ideologically approved behavior can appear on the printed page.

On another level Yiddish — or the study of Yiddish — thrives in the academy, where the full range of Yiddish literature, now a thousand years old, is analyzed with the latest tools of literary criticism. There, at least, every Yiddish sentence is not supposed to end in a joke. The irony of this situation is that where once Hebrew was the rarefied language of the learned few and Yiddish the language of the masses, now the situation is reversed. Hebrew is the daily language of six million Israelis, and Yiddish is relegated to the remote reaches of the university. Despite its hothouse existence, the full range of Yiddish and the culture out of which it grew are being given a new life. What is developing, then, are two branches of Yiddish: that of the Haredim, a spoken language without memory, without reference to the brilliant century of secular writing that is now being rediscovered; and the new treatment of Yiddish among scholars. In the universities, for the first time since the Yiddish Scientific Institute flourished in Vilna between 1925 and the onset of World War II, the study of Yiddish continues the modern linguistic tradition, analyzing regional sound shifts and dialectical variations and placing its literature in its social and historical context. The language we hear at Yiddish conferences is neither the pure Yiddish of the fishwife in the Minsk market, nor the constricted dialect of the Haredim. It is a new, bloodless, grammatically correct Yiddish. On the *Mendele* Website, which tracks the latest trends in Yiddish, this issue has caught the attention of contributors, one of whom suggested in the summer of 2005 that Yiddish be taught in one of its many dialect forms so that it would at least have the semblance of life. Yet with all its deficiencies, as a guarantee of the survival and cultivation of Yiddish, this careful new language is our last, best hope.

Inventing a Yiddish Theater in America

T he Yiddish theater in America actually began in the city of Jassy in Romania on an October evening in 1876, when Abraham Goldfaden read his poems in the wine garden of the Green Tree tavern. Goldfaden's name was well known to the frequenters of the wine garden, since the popular local singer at the tavern, Israel Grodner, often performed his poems and songs. But Goldfaden in person was a shock for this working-class Jewish audience. He appeared in a frock coat, tall silk hat, and glacé kid gloves and began by reading earnestly a long philosophical poem, "Dos Pintele Yid" (The Essential Jew). Mistaking the lack of applause after his reading for an audience overwhelmed by emotion, he continued with other works until he was finally driven from the stage by boos and whistles. As he himself recorded the event, it was a "fiasco."[1] Nonetheless, it was from this fiasco that the Yiddish theater was born. After taking counsel with Grodner, who understood his audience intimately, Goldfaden realized that what was wanted was not philosophy but homely entertainment.

In a Jewish world that was almost entirely shaped by close religious observance and dominated by the rule of rabbis of varying sects, Goldfaden had had an unusual education. Traditionally, Jewish boys were sent off to their first schoolroom as early as three years of age. There they were essentially inducted into their obligations as a religious Jew. They learned to read Hebrew, to recite the prayers that punctuated the day of every Jewish man and woman as well as the service in the synagogue. At later stages, they read the Torah in Hebrew, translating it sentence by sentence into Yiddish, and finally they reached the stage of studying the commentaries and themselves engaging in disputations about the meaning of the text. This was a long course of study — ideally lasting a lifetime. But poor children were taken out of school as early as eleven in order to begin their apprenticeship, and girls were customarily taught Yiddish at home by their mothers without the benefit of any formal schooling. In the traditional schools, no secular subjects entered the curriculum. There was no history, literature, science, or mathematics or even instruction in the languages of the countries in which they lived. Jewish children couldn't read the Cyrillic of Russia, for example, or the Latin alphabet of Poland and Romania. Enterprising youngsters taught themselves, or in well-to-do households their parents hired tutors to acquaint them with the secular learning that would be useful in the larger world.

The Jewish Enlightenment

Goldfaden was born in 1859 into an "Enlightened" family, as it would have been described then. The word "Enlightened" in those days was not neutral but described a serious dissident movement in Judaism. The Jewish Enlightenment, which began in Germany in the eighteenth century, was led by Moses Mendelssohn, and there its emphasis was on inclusiveness — the reconciliation of German culture and the traditions of Jewish learning. It took on a very different quality in eastern Europe almost a century later, where it was known by its Hebrew name, *Haskalah.* A young man who joined the movement, a *Maskil,* was taking a serious step. By adopting modern European dress, as being Enlightened implied, by going about clean-shaven and neglecting to wear a head covering indoors or at table (as Yaffe does in the first act of *The Jewish King Lear*), the young Maskil was proclaiming his distance from the traditional community. Not only did this seem to religious Jews a first step toward apostasy, it was also unequivocally "wicked" in the words of the Passover Haggadah. This little book is read during the Passover evening ceremony (Seder) and is devoted to telling the story of the exodus of the Jews from Egypt with commentaries and related anecdotes. At the beginning, the text counsels the father as to how he is to answer the questions of his sons: the simple son, the wise son, and also the wicked son. But what constitutes his wickedness? It is not that he has stolen or murdered, but that he has separated himself from the community. This is his sole crime, but it is enough. He asks, "What does all this mean to *you*?" The Haggadah text deals severely with this question: "And because he says 'to *you*' . . . he removes himself from the community, and in so doing he denies God. And therefore, in return, you must set his teeth on edge and say, 'It is because of that which God did for *me* when I came out of Egypt.' For me and not for him. Had the wicked son been there, he would not have been redeemed."

In eastern Europe, the Maskilim were leaving traditional Jewish re-ligious practice — sometimes out of loss of faith, but as often out of a desire for the delights of secular learning and the life of the secular world. But they were not leaving the Jewish world. In the West the Maskilim had brought the tools of Western scholarship to the sacred texts. But in east-ern Europe, the Maskilim wanted to use the Jewish languages — Hebrew and Yiddish — for new and secular purposes. At the same time, they were eager to acquaint themselves with Western civilization. The price these young men paid for breaking out of the conventions of Jewish society was enormous. A brilliant yeshiva student, acclaimed and honored in Jewish learned circles, at the age of eighteen would be rewarded with a rich bride and cosseted for the rest of his life. When he left this closed world he discovered that he was totally helpless to negotiate the Russian university system. His lifetime of learning was simply useless, irrelevant. Barely able to read Cyrillic script, never having studied mathematics, with no knowl-edge of history or geography or European languages — either the classics or their modern descendants — he was in a desperate situation if he hoped to enter the university. In order to pass the entrance examinations he would have to cram into two or three years the twelve or more years than any ordinary boy had spent to reach that point. And the irony was that most of these students supported themselves by teaching traditional re-ligious subjects to the children of well-to-do secular Jewish families.

No less arduous was the route taken by the Maskilim who turned their fervor for change to revolutionizing Hebrew, to making it into a secu-lar instrument for the expression of modern secular ideas and emotions. Above all they hoped to influence their as yet unenlightened brethren still lost in empty ritual and ignorant of the wide world. This enthusiasm, in-deed, sense of obligation, to enlighten others was, as we shall see, a constant theme among the first writers and actors in the Yiddish theater as well. But the Maskilim soon discovered that their passionate outpourings in their Hebrew periodicals only reached one another. The great majority of Jews had learned to read the prayer books by rote but could not understand the

Hebrew they were reciting. As the secular writers realized very quickly, if they wanted to reach their fellow Jews they would have to write in Yiddish. It was only after the middle of the nineteenth century, then, that Yiddish became a serious literary language in the hands of the three founding fathers of modern Yiddish literature. Shalom Jacob Abramowitsch—better known by his pen name Mendele Mocher Sforim, "Mendele the Book Seller"—was called the grandfather of Yiddish literature. He wrote novels and short stories in an elegant, secular style, using the persona of an itinerant bookseller. I. L. Peretz, among his other works of fiction, recreated and retold Yiddish folktales and fables for a sophisticated modern reader. Sholem Aleichem captured authentic Yiddish colloquial language in his pointed tales of ordinary life and through his irony transformed them into social commentary. Sholem Aleichem's work continues to hold a place in mainstream American culture today through the frequent revivals of *Fiddler on the Roof,* based on his Tevye stories.

Unshackled from strict obedience to Jewish religious law, the Maskilim were seen by their fellow Jews as practically heretics. Their skepticism about the minutiae of Jewish observance, their avid cultivation of the civilization and languages of Europe, their promotion of a new nationalist politics for Jews, all made them outsiders to the closed life of traditional Jews, a life bounded by religious duties, by the learning of the Torah and the commentaries, and by the eternal longing for Zion, which would be realized when the Messiah came. Of course, Jews in the Russian Empire had good cause for being suspicious of secularism. They lived under constant pressure from the tsarist regime to convert. Nicholas I, who was particularly determined to eliminate the Jewish blot of apostasy from his country, instituted a new system of army recruitment in 1827, a year after he ascended the throne. Jewish boys as young as twelve years of age were to be drafted into the army and forced to serve for twenty-five years. Far from home and familiar community, these children gradually lost all attachment to their Judaism, as Nicholas intended; many converted, married non-Jewish women, and in the course of time even lost their mother tongue. The few who returned to their homes were strange creatures, speaking a rough, broken mixture of Russian and Yiddish: at home nowhere, they were despised Jews among the Russians and strange, Russified heathen to their fellow Jews. Accounts of conscripts who returned to their villages are full of details of their discomfort with the requirements of the traditional life after their years in another world. And not a few of them left.[2]

Abraham Goldfaden, known as "the father of Yiddish theater."
(Archives of the YIVO Institute for Jewish Research)

This cruel law was abrogated in 1856, but its memory lingered, giving Jews in Russia a horror of military service. As a milder form of temptation to lure Jews out of their communities, the Russian government set up Crown Schools for Jewish children. The great inducement to send one's child to such a school was that his term of army service was shortened. However, in addition to traditional Jewish learning, these schools offered a wide array of secular subjects, all of which were regarded with suspicion by religious Jews, who saw them as the first step to a religious conversion. Goldfaden's father, a Maskil, wanted a good secular education for his son and promptly sent him to a Crown School. This led, at the next level, to a so-called Rabbinical Academy, which taught traditional Jewish subjects of higher learning: the Scriptures, the commentaries, Jewish law, rhetoric, Hebrew and Chaldean languages, and Jewish folklore. In the secular branch the candidates studied Russian and German language and literature, mathematics, physics, astronomy, and geography.[3] And while few Jewish communities would accept a rabbi with a degree awarded by a tsarist academy, teachers were far more acceptable. When Yaffe in *The Jewish King Lear* is described as someone attending the Rabbinical Academy in Vilna, the audience at once understood that he was a Maskil and was probably aiming to be a teacher in a Crown School.

The fear of conversion, marked as it had been by compulsion and the horror at those who yielded, was a major force in keeping Jewish life as narrow and traditional as possible. Every modern innovation was suspect as being only the first step toward a total break. Thus the Maskil was seen by traditional Jews as a dangerous force. With his clean-shaven face, uncovered head, and modern dress — why, just as he stood, he had already violated a dozen laws. We can see, then, how Yaffe would be regarded with such apprehension by the household of Dovidl Moysheles, the Jewish King Lear, as he comes to regard himself.

Under these circumstances, it is remarkable how enthusiastically the newborn Yiddish theater was received. By its very nature, it transgressed many customs and regulations. Whether the performances took place in taverns or restaurants, as they did at first, or in theaters, men and women sat together at tables or in seats next to one another — an impermissible practice to Orthodox Jews. Although in its first years men played women's parts, by 1880 women were regular members of the company (another violation), singing and dancing as well as acting on the stage. In its early years the Yiddish theater would not perform on Friday nights or until the end of the Sabbath on Saturday. But gradually even this gesture fell into disuse. To a community whose only exposure to theater had been the once-a-year performances at Purim by amateur groups, with men playing the women's parts, the secular theater — comedies, fantasies with songs, dances, costumes, music — was a wonderful and deliciously illicit innovation in their lives.

But parallel to the programmatic path of the Maskilim, who in any case were only a tiny part of the population, there was a strong non-ideological drift toward secularism that helped the burgeoning theater. It was perhaps most visible in the big cities, where life was less constrained by the ruling religious ethos. Odessa, on the Black Sea, was a notorious example of the new ways. It was well known for its gaiety, famous for its beautiful acacia-lined boulevards (breathtaking to new arrivals from the muddy alleys of the typical Jewish shtetl), for its theaters, its thriving night life, and devotion to pleasure. That Jewish community's fall away from religious practice was described by one historian: "Ninety percent of the city's Jewish-owned shops were . . . open on the Sabbath; Jews carried money on Saturdays, chatted in cafés and when rushing off to recite the mourner's prayer, put out their still smoldering cigarettes on the synagogue's outer walls."[4] It was also the city that drew young men eager to make their fortunes, like the unlucky Menakhem-Mendl in Sholem Aleichem's Tevye stories, who goes to Odessa hoping to get rich playing the stock market. It also drew Jacob Adler, as a young aspiring actor and enthusiastic participant in Odessa's nightlife. Later a great star of the Yiddish stage in New York, he came to Odessa hoping to find a start in one of the theaters. According to the old Jewish saying, Odessa was the ultimate place for the total fulfillment of life's pleasure: "He lives," one would say, "like God in Odessa."

The Birth of Yiddish Theater

It is no wonder that Odessa, given its easy atmosphere, should have become one of the first centers of Yiddish theater. After touring the provinces in Romania, Goldfaden finally settled in Odessa, where he produced his play *Shmendrik,* which became an enduring favorite on the Yiddish stage. The name of the hero, in fact, entered Yiddish as one of many nouns that describe a helpless, hapless, clumsy fool. Goldfaden's education, which had given him a secure understanding of both traditional

Jewish learning and the modern world, made him the perfect man to experiment with this new medium.

After the Crown School, Goldfaden went on to the Rabbinical Academy at Zhitomir, which he attended between 1857 and 1866. His musical talent came to the fore in the cantorial branch of his rabbinic studies, where he showed himself to be a fine singer. The group at Zhitomir was enterprising and in 1862 decided to put on one of the earliest of the secular Yiddish plays, *Serkele*, by Shloyme Etinger. Since this was an all-male school, the men played the women's roles, and Goldfaden won the lead as Serkele, or Little Sarah. The play was such a hit that the company took it on tour to various other academies. The production gave Goldfaden a permanent and powerful interest in the theater. Although Jews for a thousand years had put on Purim plays, the theme (with variations) was the triumph of the Jewish queen Esther and her uncle Mordechai over the bloody stratagems of Haman at the court of King Ahasuerus. One of the first plays produced by a member of the Haskalah in eastern Europe, *Di genarte Velt* (The Fooled World), which was published in 1820, was at once a comedy and a polemic against brokered marriages and Hasidism, favorite targets not only of the Maskilim, but also of the popular tavern singers. *Serkele*, written in 1830, had a more domestic plot, turning on the misdeeds of an evil sister, Serkele, who mistreats her niece, steals her jewels, etc. until the girl's father returns and sets all right. It was not published until after Etinger's death, although it came to be well known. Since the censor prohibited its publication in Russia, it did not appear in print until 1861 with the obviously fictitious place of publication given as Johannesburg, and then again in 1875 in Warsaw, but without the author's name.[5] Until then, however, it was widely circulated in manuscript form or simply read aloud at gatherings, as it had been at the Zhitomir Academy. The Maskilim, as the dissidents in Jewish society, found themselves at home in the world of the theater, a world full of skepticism toward Jewish society and ready to mock the conventional institutions. Not surprisingly, many of the first actors in the infant Jewish theater were Maskilim. Other young people, who may have been less well educated and wanting in ideology but who were good singers or had a talent for comedy, were also drawn to the new Yiddish theater. Many of the early singers in the Yiddish theater, in fact, came from the choirs of the great synagogues, which were notoriously lacking in piety.

The origins of the Yiddish theater in the wine cellars and cafés of Romania were entirely secular — in its topics, in personnel, in atmosphere, and in its audiences. Even the subject matter of the songs drew upon a certain irreverence about stock figures of Jewish life: the illiterate grandmother, the conniving matchmaker, the Hasid, the pious but hypocritical rich man. In these cafés with their makeshift stages, the informal programs gradually morphed into more elaborate presentations, as songs were performed as little playlets with the actor/singer appearing in costume and makeup. How rudimentary these presentations were can be surmised from a contemporary account that reported the actors used the carbon of burnt matches to draw lines on their faces.

A song called "The Thief," for example, was preceded by a pantomime in which a Jew is shown getting ready to go to bed. He says his nighttime prayers, gets into bed, and extinguishes the light. Enter the thief, who fills his bag with valuables; but just as he is about to escape the Jew wakes up and makes an outcry. The thief runs away but is caught by the police and brought back to the bedroom. Then, at last, he sings his song, "The Thief," a heartrending tale of the sad life that brought him to such a pass.

Some entertainments were arranged as duets or trios with such favorites as a quarrel between a husband and a wife or "The Struggle between the Hasid and the Daytsh," in which the Daytsh is understood to be a German Jew who represents the Enlightenment.[6] We can see, then, that Yaffe in Gordin's *Lear* was a type with a long history in the Yiddish theater.

Goldfaden moved the world of entertainment from these little skits to full-fledged plays. The stages on which these plays were performed were hardly less primitive than those of the cafés — but Goldfaden wrote libretti, composed music, and assembled a company, picking up new talent wherever he went. His company introduced the first woman to the Yiddish stage, Sophie Karp, who ran away from home to join his ensemble on the promise of marriage by one of the actors.[7] She was later a great success in New York, playing important roles in Boris Thomashefsky's company. Goldfaden's plays were instantly popular and remained so for decades because he both renewed and drew upon a rich folk tradition of stories populated by ghosts and spirits and moved by supernatural events, strange coincidences, and overall the hand of God. Goldfaden learned from his experience and came to understand his audience perfectly. He knew the legends that nourished their thoughts, their beliefs in the Evil Eye, in the efficacy of counterspells, in the ubiquitous presence of evil spirits, in the possibility of sudden rescues, and in a Divine Providence that saw to it that good prevailed and evil was vanquished.

After touring through Romania, Goldfaden returned to Russia and made a start in Odessa, where he took on the young Jacob Adler, then just beginning his acting career. In 1880 Goldfaden wrote one of his most enduring hits, *Shulamis,* wherein he found the formula for the musical in the grand style. By giving his characters biblical names and using a vague Eretz Israel and an even vaguer Jerusalem as the setting for his plot, he heightened a simple story of love forgotten — tragedy — and then love renewed, bringing his audience to a happy ending and sending them home whistling his tunes. One of the most famous songs to come out of *Shulamis* was "Raisins and Almonds," which Goldfaden adapted from a well-known lullaby, "Unter Yankeles Vigele" (Under Yankel's Cradle).[8] This kind of borrowing was to become a feature of the new Yiddish musical theater: composers not only freely used Yiddish folk sources and synagogue music, but also took arias from well-known European operas and later from American popular tunes. *Shulamis* was such a hit that the company even played on Friday nights until the Orthodox Jews in Odessa threatened violence. Goldfaden toured with *Shulamis* through the provinces; eventually his company played in Moscow, where they also put on *Shmendrik* to the malicious delight of the non-Jewish members of the audience, who immediately took up the name as a form of contemptuous greeting for any Jew they met on the street. This unexpected result led the Jewish intellectuals of Moscow to attack Goldfaden for bringing shame on the Jewish community. His formula for operettas was so successful, however, that two contemporary playwrights of musicals, Joseph Lateiner and Moyshe Hurwitz, found themselves no longer alone but part of a wave. They too used pseudobiblical styles, but also moved on to more contemporary plots. In 1885 Lateiner was the first to write a play set in America when he wrote on the most burning subject of the day; he called his play *The Emigration to America.*[9]

The new Yiddish theater was only one sign of the growing secularism in the Jewish world. The expanding industrialism, the new ease of movement (thanks to railroads and steam-driven ships), and the lure of America all combined to loosen the grip of the old, unchanging theocratic elders. One did not have to go so far as to stub out one's cigarette on the synagogue wall on the Sabbath. But more and more, men — and women

—going to work in the factories and workshops wore modern clothes. Men chose to be clean-shaven except for the frequently dashing moustache, and women looked more and more askance at the requirement of a shaven head and a wig after marriage.

The New World

By the middle of the nineteenth century, the nationalism stirring across Europe was giving a new focus to the thinking of young Jews in the Russian Empire. Freeing themselves from the eternal questions of law and precedent in the sacred writings, they too began to see the Jews as a nation with a national language and suddenly with a living and present-minded claim to the land of their fathers. They were no longer willing to wait until the end of Time, till the coming of the Messiah, to return to their land. At least three political movements won adherents because of these feelings: Zionism, Bundism, and Socialism. What the three movements had in common was their creation of a secular ferment in the Jewish world, a world which until now had been divided only by the religious squabbles of different sects. Rationalist Jews known as Misnagdim, who insisted that the true word could be found in close study of the Torah, warred endlessly with the adherents of a more mystical Judaism known as Hasidism, whose followers threw themselves enthusiastically into the cult of one or another charismatic "rebbe," or leader, while within the Hasidic movement there was friction between the followers of rival rebbes.

In the looser atmosphere of the United States (or, as it was called by the ultrareligious of eastern Europe, the *trayfe medina,* the unclean land) vaguer, less ideological sentiments prevailed. The old party allegiances had crossed the ocean but lost power in the new atmosphere. In the absence of the tsarist police or fear of conscription or the possibility of a pogrom, the old party programs no longer seemed directly relevant to the new concerns of a new life. But where these concerns did find both an echo and a confirmation was in the Yiddish theater. In America, the supernatural receded in daily practice. There were medicines that cured illnesses and hospitals that relieved and treated serious problems, all of which competed seriously with amulets, prayers, and spells. Life was simply less arbitrary and unpredictable. But the beliefs remained firmly embedded in Yiddish speech — no report on a fortunate event, for example, could go unpunctuated by an automatic "May no Evil Eye befall him." It was not only folk beliefs that were altered in emphasis in America; the more pro-grammatic ideologies of Socialism, Bundism, and Zionism also under-went a sea change. Harnessed to the industrial machine in the New World, the new immigrants developed a strong working-class consciousness that expressed itself in trade unionism rather than in the more radical Socialism of the Old World. Zionism also was transmuted from a movement whose members planned to settle in Eretz Israel to a rather vaguer sense of eternal connection to the Land (as it was called) together with a pride in the long history of the Jewish people. The connection to the land of their ancestors, too, was embedded in the language; to express the notion that something was too long, one said, "As long as the Jewish exile."

In America, although Jews were no longer threatened by an endemic anti-Semitism which could explode into violence at any moment, the im-migrants still remained outsiders in a Protestant, English-speaking coun-try where the Anglo-Saxon ideal reigned supreme. Yet they knew that in America, they could become Americans. In eastern Europe, no matter how many generations had lived in those lands, the Jews would never be Poles or Russians, but always "Yids" — an enduring pejorative. But in America it was enough to look like an American. One didn't aspire to sound like one or, God forbid, eat their food or engage in their way of life. But one could live in peace and security; one could seek out one's own kind for companionship and pleasure. Yet, however many of Judaism's intricate laws and customs they may have abandoned, the new immigrants could not separate themselves — nor did they want to — from their essential Jew-ishness. They may have traveled from the medieval world of the shtetl to a modern, technologically advanced society, but what united them — whatever their politics, whatever their level of religious observance — was the powerful idea of Yidishkayt, Jewishness, which held its followers in an ineradicable bond of history and language.

Emigration

The pogroms that started in Russia in April 1881, following the assas-sination of Tsar Alexander II in March, lasted until the following sum-mer; they were marked by killing, raping, and looting, especially in the Ukraine. As if this was not enough, in the following year the government enacted the May Laws, which placed further restrictions on the Jews, limiting their admission to the university and finally expelling them from

Moscow. These events were the final signal to the Jews that there was nothing good for them to be expected from life in the Russian Empire. As the correspondent for *Hameliz,* the Hebrew newspaper in Kovno, reported in April 1882, Jews were departing en masse: "Yesterday . . . two hundred families passed Kovno en route to the United States, and tomorrow thirty families are leaving from our own city."[10] From 1881 to 1924, when the U.S. government imposed restrictions on immigration, more than two and a half million Jews left eastern Europe for the United States. To put it more plainly, one in three Jews gave up on life in his birthplace. Unlike many other immigrants who came to the United States to make their fortune and then return home, the Jews came to stay. Burdened with so many memories of persecution and degradation, they felt their place of birth was not their homeland in the sense it was for other immigrants. There was no nostalgia for lost forests and fields, for quaint city streets. In fact, few ever returned even for a sentimental visit.

The Jews were different from other immigrant groups in another important way: a third of those who came after 1881 were children under the age of sixteen.[11] But they did not come as part of a family group; they came alone, entrusted when they arrived to the care of a sibling or a relative who had already settled into American life. They were not coming to families who lived in affluence. These were largely working-class people, just barely getting by themselves, and most of these youngsters went to work as soon as the law permitted them to do so and sometimes earlier. Work was nothing new for them. Many had been apprenticed from the time they were ten or eleven, and they arrived in the United States with the rudiments of a craft already in hand. As part of the transfer to a new life, the demanding practices of Jewish religious observance were very soon put to the test. The question of the Sabbath, for example, one of the most serious obligations of a pious Jew, almost immediately became an issue. If the new immigrant's job was in a factory that worked on the Sabbath, what was he to do? Should he give up his job and imperil his livelihood? Or should he make his peace with the exigencies of the modern world?

Other changes were quickly undertaken, freely and even defiantly. As they had begun to do in the Old Country, most immediately abandoned old country dress for American clothes. Men shaved their beards. Women who had been shorn of their hair as brides allowed it to grow again and enjoyed new fashions in hats instead of the inevitable kerchief worn over a wig. Attendance at the *mikvah*, the ritual bath in which married women immersed themselves a week after the cessation of their menstrual period, also fell drastically. Unlike the Maskilim of the Old World, who had elaborate theories to explain their choices, these young people simply followed what seemed to be the natural steps both to survival and enjoyment of the New World to which they had come.

The rule of custom and authority suddenly lost its force. When a girl of sixteen could earn her own living — and did — she no longer could be subjected to an arranged marriage against her will. In the New World many of these girls no longer lived in a tightly knit family subject to the authority of their father. As boarders with relatives or countrymen, they had a new independence. The arranged marriage was perhaps one of the first institutions to go in America. Living outside the conventional family, working girls were not passively sitting at home waiting for the *shadkhn*, or matchmaker, to arrive with his list of prospective bridegrooms. Since these girls lived out in the world, going to work, going to night school, going to the theater, to dances, they met many possible suitors, and love matches became the rule rather than the exception.

In discussions of arranged marriages the girl is usually depicted as the victim, but the young men, or even boys, were also harmed by the system. Young boys barely out of adolescence were often chosen as bridegrooms for their luster as students and then brought into an arranged marriage, unprepared either for life or for marriage. One Maskil, Benjamin Feigenbaum, a writer who later moved to New York, wrote a song to describe his feeling about his arranged marriage. It was titled "They bound me with a stone on my neck and threw me into the ocean." Writers of Haskalah literature often emphasized how unready and incompetent they were in meeting women and finding someone to love. Mica Yosef Berdichevsky, who was born in Medzibezh in the Ukraine into a family of Hasidic rabbis, nonetheless went west and in 1896 earned a doctorate in philosophy at the University of Bern. He became known as a novelist writing in both Hebrew and Yiddish. In his Hebrew novel *A Raven Flies,* he gives us some insight into the feelings of a yeshiva-bred young man when he gets out into the world. "In my stunted maturity," he writes,

> I lacked a natural prompting that would tell me that *this* is the woman made for me. . . . On Sunday mornings when my secret yearnings forced me from my room and my books into the throng, and stunned I made my solitary way among the crowds of men and women promenading through

the gay boulevards, most of them couples arm-in-arm and exuding a sense of togetherness — it was then that I conceived a great envy of all those complacent souls. . . . I recalled that in my father's world inside the Pale love comes only after solemnizing a marriage under the four poles of the *hupah*. . . . Intimacy with a woman with an exalted soul is the only thing I understand and seek, a perfect soul whom I could love with all my heart.[12]

While this was more exalted language than that of the working men and boys who made up the overwhelming majority of the immigrants, it nonetheless described the restriction that both men and women felt about approaching one another in the Old Country. But America was a new world, where they could behave freely. At home it was a sin even to look at a woman. In the popular dancing schools in New York, a man could put his arm around a strange woman's waist. Who knew any longer what was a transgression?

If Jews could go to work on the Sabbath, they could certainly go to the theater as well! And the Yiddish theaters in New York had no hesitation about giving five performances on the weekend, one on Friday night and two each on Saturday and Sunday. These were, in fact, the most lucrative nights of the week. The Yiddish theater arrived in the United States, along with the high tide of Jewish emigration from Russia, because it had also been targeted by the tsarist government. In September of 1883 the Russian government prohibited performances in Yiddish, and some speculated that the decree had been occasioned by an inflammatory antigovernment speech in the prologue to Goldfaden's new play, *Bar Kochba*.[13] The actors were dismayed and at first sought ways of circumventing the decree by advertising that they were presenting plays in German. And indeed, they did speak a strange kind of Yiddish that was denatured of its own rhythms and with German vocabulary substituted at various points. This hybrid language, called Daytshmerish, that was never spoken anywhere but onstage persisted for several decades and was even transported to the Yiddish theater in New York.

In America, the young, naïve population of Jewish immigrants streamed to the Yiddish theater on weekends, making it their own with a passion that caught the attention of the American visitors and theater critics who came to see this new phenomenon. These young people, as yet unburdened by family obligations, had the time and the enthusiasm for this dazzling phenomenon. Even poorly paid workers could afford the twenty-five cents that would buy them a seat in the balcony. Avid and frequent theatergoers, they formed fan clubs that cheered their heroes in the theater and sometimes came to blows with one another in the street. Stars such as Boris Thomashefsky and Jacob Adler were often showered with flowers and besieged at the stage door by their admirers. This was particularly true of Thomashefsky, who specialized in dazzling romantic roles designed especially to win the hearts of the women in the audience.

Hutchins Hapgood, a New York journalist writing in 1902, gives a vivid report on his visits:

> On [weekend] nights the theater presents a peculiarly picturesque sight. Poor workingmen and women with their babies of all ages fill the theater. Great enthusiasm is manifested, sincere laughter and tears accompany the sincere acting on the stage. Pedlars of soda-water, candy, of fantastic gewgaws of many kinds mix freely with the audience between the acts. . . . Many a poor Jew, man or girl, who makes no more than $10 a week in the sweatshop, will spend $5 of it on the theater, which is practically the only amusement of the Ghetto Jew. . . . It is not only to see the play that the poor Jew goes to the theater. It is to see his friends and the actors. With these latter he, and more frequently she, try in every way to make acquaintance, but commonly are compelled to adore at a distance.[14]

What They Saw

The Yiddish theater may have been born in Romania and passed its adolescence in Russia, but it grew up in New York. After the theaters in Russia were closed in 1883, the actors scattered to various cities in Europe with a Yiddish-speaking population: Berlin, Paris, London. But the real mecca was New York. All of Europe seemed to be moving to New York. And the actors followed their public. In the mass exodus of Jews from eastern Europe after 1881, 90 percent of the emigrants chose to come to the United States, and the majority remained where they landed, in New York. By 1915 nearly 1,400,000 Jews were living in New York City, providing a vast audience for the thriving Yiddish culture, a culture which produced 150 periodicals in the years between 1885 and 1914, where special cafes and restaurants catered to the "intelligentsia," and where of course everyone went to the theater.[15]

Especially to the community of young, naïve immigrants, the secular theater was a thrilling, seductive innovation. The first theater companies were hardly better trained than the amateur Purim players, but what they lacked in training they made up for in enthusiasm and natural talent. Even the condescending American theater critic Norman Hapgood recognized this force when he wrote, "My trips to the Ghetto give me more to think about and less reason to regret time ill spent than most of my theater evenings on Broadway."[16] There was a quality of intimacy between audience and actors that was lacking "Uptown" and led to a vehemently interactive theatrical experience. "For the impoverished playgoer," one critic wrote, "the early Yiddish drama halls and clubs inspired the same devotion as synagogues and the playwrights were viewed with the same admiration and awe as the most famous rabbis."[17] Audiences were outspoken in their response to the action on the stage, and the actors replied with equal fervor with speeches before the curtain between acts. They frequently appeared at the end of the play to announce a new production or not infrequently to denounce a rival's play running in another theater.

Jacob Gordin's plays were particularly apt to arouse passionate feelings since they dealt with "realistic" situations and had characters who aroused instantaneous feelings of hatred, pity, fury, etc. One often-told story occurred in a performance in Montreal by Adler during the third act of *The Jewish King Lear* when Dovidl Moysheles (the Lear figure) is being starved by his daughter, and his wife cannot unlock the kitchen cabinets to bring him some food. As he sits on the stage, fainting with hunger, a member of the audience runs down the aisle calling out to him by his Yiddish name: "Just forget about her, Yankl, that wicked woman. You can see that today you'll never get a bite to eat from her. She has a stone instead of a heart. Spit on her, Yankl, and come to me. My wife will make you such a supper that you will enjoy every bit of it. Come, Yankl! May she choke, that rotten daughter of yours. Come to me."[18]

Gordin himself tells of an encounter with a member of the audience who also was mystified by illusion and the apparent reality:

After the first performance of *Kenig*, I heard an old Jew say, "A good piece. It gives us a model of how to live."

"I thank you," I said to him with pleasure.

"Why are you so happy about it?" the Jew asked me.

"I am the author," I answered the Jew.

"What do you mean 'author'?" asked the Jew.

"I *wrote* it," I said trying to make it clear to him.

"Why would you have had to write it, since the actors are speaking it freely? They know it by heart." The Jew still couldn't understand the relationship between the play and r⸱⸱ [19]

Boaz Young, an actor who was later a member of Adler's company, did not try to come to the aid of the hero when, as a teenager, he saw his first play, Goldfaden's *Bar Kochba*. But he was overwhelmed by the sets, the costumes, and especially the charms of the leading lady. "All of this together," he wrote, "carried me away to another world. I forgot that I was sitting in the Eldorado Theater in Warsaw, and believed that I found myself on the high mountain in Zion and was seeing everything in reality."[20]

When the Yiddish theater began in America in 1882, it had no competition. As yet there were no movies; the immigrants could not understand the American theater, and sports were equally incomprehensible. There was, however, one major problem. The Yiddish theater had no repertoire. As an art form in the Yiddish-speaking world, it was so new that Goldfaden's plays were its first and almost the only resource. Fortunately Goldfaden was an immensely prolific writer who set the model for the playwrights who followed him. Of Goldfaden's two modes, his elevated or heroic mode — in which he took his plot from biblical episodes, such as Judah HaMacabee, or from the exploits of great figures in Jewish history, such as Bar Kochba, who led the last Jewish revolt against the Romans between 132 and 135 C.E. — was the style most often imitated in America. This heroic mode permitted the extravaganzas that were so dear to the Yiddish theatergoer's heart. These were highly wrought productions with noble protagonists in gaudily elaborate costumes, with singers, dancing girls, chariots drawn by real horses, and every possible effect to dazzle a young and innocent audience. Bessie Thomashefsky, Boris Thomashefsky's wife and an important actress in his company, wrote with amusement in her memoirs about her husband's appearance in his most famous role, *Alexander, Crown Prince of Jerusalem,* in which he enters on a white horse. "The audience was utterly delighted," she writes, "with the horse."[21]

These plays, called *shund,* or "trash," with a wrinkle of the nose by the Yiddish intelligentsia, were nonetheless the darlings of the working-class audience, who were not too sophisticated to be enchanted by the effects. But more than that, it was not only the circus atmosphere of lights, tights, and music — it was also a time for these young people to feel proud of themselves. Having come from a life of fear, humiliation, and deprivation, they gloried in the image of themselves as heroic and glamorous figures.

Boris Thomashefsky, who was a prodigious producer and star of these types of plays, describes in his autobiography his costume for the role of King Charles IX in *The Huguenots:* he wore "golden clothes with a gold cloak, a diamond collar with a gold cross, set with glittering stones."[22] But he was not alone. The actors in the Yiddish theater competed with one another in the splendor of their costumes and staging. Thomashefsky described the competition with remarkable objectivity:

"The Yiddish stage at that time," he said, "depended entirely on Lateiner and Hurwitz [whose plays called for elaborate costuming]. Tights with golden crowns and bare arms, revealing decolleté wrapped in silken cloaks were what all the stars wore. The difference was only in colors. If [David] Kessler wore a large hat on stage with a long feather, with bare feet and a shirt with red beads; then Adler wore an even larger hat with three feathers and wrapped himself in a golden shawl adorned with gold coins. Also with bare feet, bare arms and a bare neck. But in order to make it even more striking, he put chains around his neck, bracelets on his arms and also a pair of Turkish earrings in a green color. In order to outdo them and to show them that I understood the art [of costume] better than they, I put on silk stockings made in three colors and instead of one cloak, I attached three cloaks to one another and wore with this a crown, sword, armor, bracelets, earrings and a turban of many colors and many kinds of cloth. Next to me they looked like common soldiers.

Then began a competition. They declaimed; I sang. If they shot, I stabbed. If they made their entrances on a horse, I came in on a golden coach drawn by a team of horses. If they had thunder, I had lightning. If it snowed at their theaters, I had rain. If Kessler sang the Prayer for Forgiveness, I sang the Mourner's Kaddish. If, at their theaters, they murdered one enemy, I murdered many and all at one blow."[23]

It was not only clothes and trappings that were used to convey the atmosphere of another world, another time. Even the language was altered in a way that was meant to separate it from everyday speech. *Daytshmerish*, the language invented in Russia to get around the prohibition of Yiddish, was used in America for these grand productions, and the prose was equally heightened. "Such pseudo-Biblical bombast," according to a historian of the Yiddish stage, "certainly glorified the Yiddish *jargon*. It glorified the spectators' identity too, as they watched Jews wearing golden robes and crowns, and speaking Yiddish with crushing dignity. It was a marvelous new experience for the proletarian immigrant community."[24] Although the actors, on the whole, found it difficult and absurd to speak in this way, the main authors of these operettas insisted on it; indeed they would have preferred German as being even more elevated. Thomashefsky found it particularly trying and complained that after an evening of declaiming in *Daytshmerish* he had a "swollen tongue."[25] Nonetheless it continued in force for more than a decade until the arrival of realism in the Yiddish theater brought plain Yiddish even to the heroic musical dramas.

Joseph Lateiner and Moyshe Hurwitz, who also followed the Yiddish theater to its new center in New York, were essentially the creators of the rich repertoire of musicals that became the hallmark of the Yiddish stage in America. But the audience was demanding and theaters were few, so that even a successful play could not be performed indefinitely. A play might run for a number of weeks or at most a season, but the audience needed something new to keep them coming back. This put Lateiner and Hurwitz under tremendous pressure to find new material — new plots, new dialogue, new music. Thomashefsky described how Lateiner borrowed freely from European drama, stringing together scenes that sometimes made no sense — at least to him. Bessie Thomashefsky was even more scornful than her husband, describing each new work Lateiner offered them as "another masterpiece." She, too, found the plots ridiculous and in her memoir tells how she responded to the opening of the play *Ezra, or the Eternal Jew:* "It was an amazing story: a certain Jew with a beard has a daughter, and they live in a forest. Where else," she asks sardonically, "does a Jew live with his daughter?"[26] The audience seemed to take no notice of these absurdities; they were totally beguiled by the glamorous scenery, the stars, and the music and did not ask for edification as long as they were entertained.

At one point Hurwitz even attempted to start an opera company by translating three popular operas, *Carmen, Faust,* and *Rigoletto,* into Yiddish and bringing over a troupe of opera singers from Europe. But it was not a success — possibly because it was too strange for the public or because the operas were presented too meagerly, with skimpy scenery and costumes and a small orchestra, and lacked the splendor that was available elsewhere in the theater. Thomashefsky had a much more categorical answer: "It is my conviction," he wrote, "that the Yiddish theater must be Jewish."[27]

The Stars

By 1890 the Yiddish theater had settled into a star system with three major actors who formed independent and competing companies: David Kessler, Jacob Adler, and Boris Thomashefsky. Kessler and Adler were the closest rivals since each was essentially a dramatic actor, and in one memorable season they even collaborated, playing Shakespeare's *Othello* and on alternate nights changing places as Othello and Iago. Thomashefsky, with his excellent voice and glamorous presence, was the unopposed king of the operetta world.

Jacob Adler's one failing — that he was not a singer — forced him to search for dramatic roles that would do justice to his acting talent and his legendary stage presence. But he denied that his choice of plays was driven by his lack of musical talent. "From my earliest years," he wrote in his auto-biography, "I have leaned toward those plays where the actor works . . . with his voice, face, eyes; not with jests and comic antics, but with the principles of art; not to amuse the public with tumbling and *salto mortales,* but to awaken in them and in himself the deepest and most powerful emotions."[28] Given the weakness of the Yiddish theater's repertoire, actors drew upon European plays — especially those with a Jewish subject — and had them translated into Yiddish. Two of the earliest translations, Karl Gutzkow's *Uriel Acosta* and Eugene Scribe's opera *La Juive (The Jewess)* with music by Jacques Halevy, were used by Adler, and *Uriel Acosta* re-mained in his repertoire for many years. Adler did not shrink from the great Shakespearean roles, and his Shylock became so famous that he was asked to perform it on the American stage. Since Adler's English was never very good, the audience was treated to a performance wherein the other actors spoke English and Adler declaimed in Yiddish. In an interview in *Theater* magazine in 1902, just before his appearance, Adler outlined his view of the role. "Shylock," he reflected, "being rich enough to forgo the interest on his three thousand ducats for the purely moral satisfaction of his revenge, such a Shylock, I say, would be richly dressed and proud of mien rather than the poor cringing figure time has made familiar. . . . The verdict, of course, goes against him. . . . But having bought so dearly the right to his contempt for his Christian enemies, would he not walk out of that courtroom head erect, the very apotheosis of defiant hatred and scorn? That is the way I see Shylock, and that is how I have played him."[29] The reviewer for the *Evening Journal* the next day gave the American verdict: "He played the character in a way never seen on the American stage and defying imitation . . . Shylock revealed as the Jew of the Ages."[30]

Thomashefsky, whose musical plays had made him rich and famous, nonetheless envied Adler's standing as a serious, intellectual actor. When he heard that Adler had announced he was going to perform Shakespeare's *Othello*, he immediately stepped before the curtain in his own theater to inform the public that he would next be appearing as Shakespeare's *Ham-let*. This required a level of preparation that strained the resources of all the members of his company. To help them master the intricacies of the play, Thomashefsky brought over the director of the German theater who was experienced in producing Shakespeare. Thomashefsky's company did put it on to such great success that on opening night the audience demanded that the playwright take a bow. They only relented when Thomashefsky stepped forward to explain that since the author lived far away, in England, he could not be present to accept their applause. Thomashefsky himself, who was a keen observer of the public as well as of the box office, had his reservations as he reflected on that first night: "Although *Hamlet* had an enormous success on the Yiddish stage, it would have been a mistake to have expected the success to last. The audience had expressed admiration and enthusiasm. But the matter of the play remained foreign and far from their ordinary preoccupations. What drew them to the theater [regularly] was something lighter, something nearer. And this same response was what happened to Adler and Kessler's *Othello*."[31] Nevertheless, *Hamlet* continued to haunt him, and eventually he wrote his own version, *Der Yeshiva Bokher* (The Yeshiva Student), which occasioned the much-quoted poster, "Shakespeare's *Hamlet* — translated and improved. Presented by Boris Thomashefsky."

Adler did not come to the United States until a decade after Thomashefsky. After the decree of 1883 banning Yiddish theater in Russia, he and his wife moved to London, where many other Russian actors settled. There they found a rudimentary Yiddish theater and a poor working-class community of immigrant Jews to support it. Some of the theaters had room for no more than one hundred people, and the largest could accommodate five hundred. Nonetheless Adler wrote warmly about this period in his life, about the intimacy between actors and audience and their loud expressions of enthusiasm with applause, shouts, and cheers. The actors earned little and lived poorly, but London drew some of the best actors of the Yiddish stage in their flight from Russia. Here Adler honed his talents, developing as a character actor in *The Beggar of Odessa*. This play was a Yiddish adaptation of a famous French play, *The Rag Pickers of Paris* by Felix Pyet.[32] But he developed his grand dramatic style as well, especially in the role of Uriel Acosta, and he also appeared in Scribe's *La Juive*, Friedrich von Schiller's *The Robbers*, and others. He drew on a vast array of European authors for plots and themes: Henrik Ibsen, Gerhart Hauptmann, Leo Tolstoy, Maxim Gorki, and, of course, Shakespeare. So great was Adler's effect on the London audience that he was called by the Hebrew name Nesher Hagodel (in its Yiddish pronunciation) — The Great Eagle — a play on the meaning of Adler.

But a disaster occurred one night when Adler's company was performing. An audience member shouted "fire" at the sight of a harmless stage fire and started a panic that led to the deaths of seventeen people. This put an end to the Jewish theater in London for a long time, and without an audience, the actors were forced to leave. Adler and his company decided on the United States, but their first visit to America was not a success, and the company broke up. In 1886 Adler returned to Europe and eventually went to Warsaw, where he played successfully for several years until he was approached by American theater managers and asked to come to New York. "When I came to America in [1890]," he writes in his autobiography, "I was an actor famous throughout the Yiddish theatrical world."[33]

But Adler was not only an actor; he was also a man with a mission. As a young aspiring actor in Odessa he had become friends with a lawyer, Yisroel Rosenberg, who was a founder of the Yiddish theater in that city. Standing in the wings with a very nervous Adler on their opening night, Rosenberg had spoken to him in a way that had a lasting effect. "Look at Spivakovsky [a member of their troupe]," said Rosenberg. "He has given up cigarettes, given up new clothes! He spends his days reading German books, learning about the theater, learning about the drama — all to make himself a worthy pioneer. And you, too, Yankele, if you mean to be an actor, a *Yiddish* actor, will have to do the same. Remember, we live in a time when Jews are being persecuted. A crisis is coming in Jewish life. Young people who adored everything Russian are turning back to their own language, their own traditions."[34] This homily gave Adler a sense of higher purpose that never left him, and it also animated some of the Russian Jewish intellectuals who came to America. The lucky ones found work on Yiddish journals, which they used as a platform from which they could reach Jewish workers. Others, like Morris Rosenfeld, the famous proletarian poet, worked in clothing factories or, like Thomashefsky in his early days, rolling cigars in tobacco workshops. Abe Cahan, one of the prominent figures in this group, was the editor of the *Jewish Daily Forward* and became a powerful voice in reviewing the Yiddish theater. But it must be said that, on the whole, the intelligentsia flocked to the mainstream theaters with far more enthusiasm than they brought to the Yiddish theater, and the actors were keenly aware of the low regard in which they were held by the literati.

Boris Thomashefsky as Hamlet.
(The Dorot Jewish Division,
The New York Public Library, Astor,
Lenox and Tilden Foundations)

In 1891, a year after Adler came to New York, Jacob Gordin left for New York to begin again in a new world. In Russia he had been a journalist for a Russian newspaper, but his political activities had put him on the tsarist police wanted list. Learning of his imminent arrest, he left Russia alone, while his wife and their nine children moved in with her parents to await the time when he could send for them. For Gordin this was an unwilling and hasty move. "Every departure," he once wrote, "is a rehearsal for a funeral. The one who leaves becomes especially dear and those whom we have lost, become ever more good and beloved."[35] And, indeed, he never stopped mourning for his lost Russia.

Whether his family was with him or in Russia, Gordin still needed money for their support. Yet the dreamer prevailed, and on the day after his arrival he wrote to the Baron de Hirsch Fund, which was dedicated to settling Jews on the land, to ask for help for himself and some fifteen families (still in Russia) who wanted to make their living as farmers in a collective enterprise. Only four of the adults whom he describes had any experience on the land. The others were a varied mixture of locksmiths, carpenters, stocking knitters, dressmakers. All, wrote Gordin, are "young, strong, mentally and morally developed." But the Baron de Hirsch Fund was not impressed and refused its help. There was nothing for Gordin to do but turn to journalism to earn a living.[36]

When he arrived in New York, he first sought work as a journalist for the Russian language newspapers. But these could employ him only irregularly and paid badly. Finally, Phillip Krantz, the editor of the Social Democratic *Arbeter Tsaytung* and a friend who also knew Adler, suggested that Gordin try his hand at writing Yiddish plays, which were always in demand and offered to bring the two men together. Gordin, who had never seen a Yiddish play in Russia, nonetheless had a poor opinion of Yiddish actors and arrived at the meeting full of apprehension. As he wrote in his memoirs, "I was very curious to see a Yiddish actor, to see what kind of an animal that is. I had the notion that if I were to write a play — the Yiddish actor would immediately play it out for me. He would first wipe his nose on his sleeve, then jump up on a bench and begin to declaim."[37]

The encounter finally took place in a wine cellar on the Lower East Side, a favorite gathering place of the Jewish intelligentsia. When the two men met, they spoke Russian to one another, always Gordin's preferred language, since he had not spoken Yiddish since he was a child. The large

group captured the attention of Boris Thomashefsky, who was also there
that night. He noticed a group of Adler's company had come in and then,
"suddenly there arrived a handsome Jew, with a large, handsome beard,
and with two [more] actors who join the others and order tea. The handsome Jew looks at them with his large, beautiful eyes and examines them.
He commands great respect." Krantz, as the *shadkhn* in this encounter,
began by reading a humorous story Gordin had just published in his
newspaper. This caught the enthusiasm of Sigmund Mogulesko, the star
comedian of the company, who immediately proposed that Gordin convert the story into a play. But Adler had larger ideas. He drew from his
pocket a book with a German play and gave it to Gordin, suggesting he
could translate it and give its main characters Jewish names; this was a
common way of creating plays for the Yiddish theater at the time. Gordin,
however, handed the book back "with a fine gesture, and said: 'No, if I
write a play, I will write a Jewish play, not a German play with Jewish
names.'"[38]

Gordin had, however, prepared for this encounter and produced a
clipping from a Russian newspaper telling the story of a man who had
been exiled to Siberia, had escaped, but was caught and sent back. That
had given Gordin the idea for a much more complicated story, one that
Adler immediately accepted and commissioned Gordin to write. This became his first play in America, called *Siberia*. At the end of the evening
Gordin had not only launched his career as a playwright in America, but
also changed his extravagant opinion about Yiddish actors. He wrote in
his memoirs about that evening, "I met with several gentlemen who not
only had silk top hats and handkerchiefs, but also talked to the point. In
the eyes of several I saw the spark of real talent and their faces were
expressive of intelligence."[39]

Although Gordin changed his mind about the actors, he was not prepared for the heavy dependence on improvisation and the lavish use of
music in the Yiddish theater. As it turned out, Gordin had to educate his
actors and also the public on how to receive his new kind of "dry" play, as
it was called since it had no music or dances. Gordin discovered the labor
that lay ahead of him when he attended the first rehearsal of *Siberia*. When
Gordin arrived for the rehearsal he found that the cast was agitated because there was no music; Kessler wanted to sing an aria in the second act,
and Mogulesco was totally dissatisfied with his role. He had too little
space for his comic tricks and wanted to insert one of his songs and a dance

to broaden his presence. Furthermore, the actors did not expect to speak his plain prose on the stage but rather had immediately converted it into *Daytshmerish* and further changed his text to make the language ridiculously high-flown. In Gordin's story, Rosenzweig, a Jew who has been condemned to prison in Siberia for some crime, escapes from his transport, goes off to a town where he is unknown, and starts a new life, a life which is threatened by a cruel antagonist. When the hero appealed for mercy to his tormentor, a scene Gordin had written with heartrending simplicity, the actors had substituted these words: "Most noble Herr Berl Taratutie, when the lion begins to roar in his cage, when the tiger snaps and springs, when the leopard tears and bites, then will the justice of heaven triumph and pure Jewish patriotic feelings will resound with 'Hear O Israel.'"[40] Gordin, who had written the play with almost religious dedication, was horrified to discover what was happening to it and took a very strong line, insisting that the actors play it as written. But tempers were aroused. There was a violent scene, several of the major actors protesting vehemently. In his anger, Mogulesco went so far as to accuse Gordin of anti-Semitism and demanded that he leave the theater. Gordin left, and Adler, taking Gordin's part, prevailed on the cast to present the play in this new way, using plain speech and plain language.

But the audience was not ready for it. On opening night the first two acts of *Siberia* were a disaster. One of the actors, Leon Blank, described later how the audience had whooped and laughed at both the play and the actors. They could not accept the fact that "the heroes spoke plain Yiddish and not *Daytshmerish* with all its ornaments. There was even lacking the expected hysterical outburst 'Almighty God is my witness.' And without the 'Almighty Witness' at that time, no play was considered complete." And other conventions were violated as well. As Blank continues, "One of the heroes, Slerovatel Saburov, is an honorable Gentile, while the pious Jew, Berl Taratutie — is an outcast, an informer, an evil man. In those times, an honorable Gentile in a Yiddish play appeared as rarely as a white crow! Especially when, standing side by side with the honorable Gentile, the pious Jew is such a disgusting person."[41]

Adler, who believed in the play, was distraught at its reception and with tears in his eyes came out after the second act to talk to the public. "'I stand before you ashamed and humiliated,' he said. 'My head is bowed in sorrow that you, dear sirs, do not understand such a masterpiece by the famous Russian writer Jacob Michailovitch Gordin. Dear Sirs, my dear sirs, if you could understand what a great work we are playing for you tonight, then you would not have laughed and shouted.' At which point Adler broke down and wept. This had a great effect on the public, which warmly applauded him."[42]

The third act went very differently from the first two. The newly attentive public was prepared to enter into the mood of the play. By the third act the hero, Rosenzweig, has become a successful shopkeeper; he is married, has a daughter, and lives a quiet, lawful life. In this town he has a competitor, Berl Taratutie, another Jew who is extremely pious and whose son is interested in the hero's daughter, a match he opposes. When Taratutie suddenly discovers Rosenzweig's secret, he decides to reveal his identity to the police. The fugitive comes to him to plead for his life: "Reb Berl Taratutie," he says, in a simple and poignant line, "why do you want to make me so wretched?" "The theater," remembers Blank, "was like a synagogue at Yom Kippur." Mogulesco had never realized how powerful a few simple words could be. As Rosenzweig's servant, he takes his farewell, and when he said his line, "Dear master, we are parting!" he himself wept and the public also. These few words in the play had such a compelling effect that Mogulesco realized Gordin had turned him from a clown into an artist. He and others in the cast wrote notes of apology to Gordin, who finally came to the third performance of his first play.

The news about this new kind of play reverberated outside the theater, as Bessie Thomashefsky wrote: "There were unsettling rumors in our little theater world that over at the Union Theater they were producing a strange play in which the actors talk like ordinary people, as they talk in their own homes and not at all the way actors are supposed to speak." But Gordin's reputation was frightening to the actors because he was reputed to be someone who knew something about the theater and was an intellectual. Bessie Thomashefsky went to see *Siberia,* and although it was a dry play she was "delighted with the prose — so simple, so human and so natural! I wished and prayed to God that Gordin would write a play for us where I would have a role, so that I, too, could talk like a human being on the stage." She also observed how not only Gordin's language, but also his stage pictures "brought the audience back home to where their cradle had stood, to where the old grandmother had sat by the hearth knitting a sock and rocking the cradle."[43]

But Bessie Thomashefsky, like her husband, had a clear sense of what worked in the theater. "At first the play did not make a great impression on

Bessie Thomashefsky, star of her husband Boris Thomashefsky's troupe.
(Archives of the YIVO Institute for Jewish Research)

the public," she observed, "(which was true of many other of Gordin's plays) because the public was simply not used to them. The audience simply didn't understand them. What kind of a theater is it," she asks in a biting reflection on her audience, "where one doesn't even stand on one's head and crow 'cock-a-doodle-do?' "[44] Although *Siberia* had a brief run, it did not escape the notice of the Orthodox press, which was incensed because the villain in the play is a pious Jew, and they denounced Gordin accordingly. This was a pattern that was to continue, and with a later play, *Hasia, the Orphan,* it actually led to open warfare.

Gordin's Plays

Gordin had an unerring sense for the problems afflicting the new immigrants. However much they loved the musicals and comedies, Gordin's plays reached them at another level. In his second play, *The Pogrom in Russia,* one of the women is raped. The pogroms had happened recently enough to have affected the members of his audience directly. The remembrance of home in this case was not nostalgia, but a remembrance of suffering that continued even in the safety of America. As one young woman wrote to the *Bintel Brief* column in the daily *Forward* asking for advice: "I was born in a small town in Russia and my mother brought me up alone. . . . A pogrom broke out and my mother was the first victim of the bloodbath. They spared no one, and no one was left but me. But that wasn't enough for the murderers, they robbed me of my honor. . . . I was alone, despondent and homeless, until relatives in America brought me over. But my wounded heart found no cure here either. . . . A few months ago, however, I met a young man, a refined and decent man. . . . He has already proposed marriage and he is now waiting for my answer. I want to marry this man, but I keep putting off giving him an answer because I can't tell him the secret that weighs on my heart."[45]

The *Bintel Brief,* a letter column in the *Forward,* became an outlet for the misfortunes and perplexities that afflicted the immigrants. Although the answers were often enough without definitive advice (as in this case), on the whole the editor took a strong line on women's rights, on the advantages of Americanization and education.

Another play by Gordin, *God, Man and Devil,* also found its echo in the *Bintel Brief.* The play was a retelling of Goethe's *Faust,* just as *Lear* had been a retelling of Shakespeare's play. Hershel, the Faust figure, is a pious but poor scribe who through the magic of the Mephistopheles figure wins the lottery and is suddenly a rich man. Mephistopheles in Gordin's play is given the name Mazik, in a wink to the audience, since it is a Yiddish word for a mischievous child, a "little devil." Mazik becomes Hershel's advisor and points out to him that he, Hershel, is committing a terrible sin every day that he lives with his wife. They have been married for twenty years, and she has not had a child. Instead they have raised the orphaned daughters of her dead sister. One of them is now seventeen and very attractive, as Hershel, in an indiscreet moment, has told Mazik. According to Jewish law, after ten years of marriage, if the wife remains barren, the man is obliged to divorce her and marry again to fulfill the injunction to "be fruitful and multiply."

This was not an arcane legalism, but a gripping dilemma to Gordin's audience. As the *Bintel Brief* testifies, it was still a source of torment. A wife who is under threat of just such a divorce writes, "I am a twenty-eight-year-old woman, married for six years, and my only trouble is that I have no children. . . . My husband eats my heart out with a few words, like rust eats iron. He keeps saying it's "nearer than farther" to the ten-year limit, when according to Jewish law, I will have to give him a divorce if I don't have a baby by that time. I can't find words to express to you how I suffer from these remarks. He's drawing my blood drop by drop and I'm sinking from day to day."[46]

In his play, Gordin makes Hershel, and the audience, choose between what is morally or legally right. This is the old Maskil way of questioning tradition. Hershel accepts Mazik's advice, and it proves to be only the first step toward his undoing. If the audience left the Lateiner and Hurwitz musicals humming, they left the Gordin plays with a great deal to think about, a great deal to discuss over a glass of tea in the after-theater cafés on Houston Street.

Although Gordin's plays, unlike the works of Lateiner and Hurwitz, were not guaranteed box office successes, they nonetheless aroused Hurwitz's indignation. Angered by Gordin's violation of the basic convention of the Yiddish theater that humble characters spoke comically and heroes spoke *Daytshmerish,* he told the playwright Leon Kobrin his views in no uncertain terms: "They're all calling for Gordin. Why Gordin? Is he a playwright? In his plays, they speak plain prose. On the stage! The same prose that they speak on the street. Have you ever heard of such a thing? He's brought Hester Street onto the stage! Even a prince, in his plays,

God, Man, and Devil at the Yiddish Art Theatre, starring Celia Adler as the niece, Maurice Schwartz as the Devil, and Lazar Freed as Hershel. (Archives of the YIVO Institute for Jewish Research)

would speak such prose! Have you ever. . . ? They're all in a commotion over Gordin's prose! Just imagine, if Gordin were to present *Hamlet, the Prince of Denmark* by Shakespeare, he would also have him speak Hester Street language." When Kobrin questions him: "How then would you have Hamlet speak on the Yiddish stage?" Hurwitz has a ready answer: "What do you mean, how should he speak? Why German is what he should speak! Have you ever seen a prince speaking Yiddish? And you want to write plays that are true to life? Well, well, show me a prince anywhere who speaks prose as they do on Hester Street." And finally, to conclude the discussion, Hurwitz offers the basis for his reasoning: "On the stage one must speak a better language, a more beautiful language, not just kitchen-language. We want to ennoble the language and make it more beautiful."[47]

Abraham Goldfaden, the father of the Yiddish theater, reflected in rather more tearful terms on the destruction Gordin was wreaking on his creation. Goldfaden, at the end of his life, had the disappointment of seeing the Yiddish stage move on from his work. When he came to America in 1902, a few years before his death, he saw two of his plays produced—one by Adler, the other by Thomashefsky. And both failed. On the occasion of this visit, Kobrin went to see Goldfaden when he was visiting Thomashefsky in his dressing room. Kobrin describes Goldfaden's grand appearance: "in a black cape which opens to reveal an immaculate snow-white shirt, with a white tie. On his hands, white gloves and on a table next to him a gleaming top-hat and a walking stick with a gilded handle." Goldfaden, always conscious of himself as the "father of the Yiddish theater," denounced Gordin's new success to Kobrin: "Look at what he has done to my child! Taken my beloved child, my Jewish child, my Benjamin, and has converted him [to Christianity]. My son who would say Kaddish for me—he has defiled him. He [Gordin] is, after all, a missionary—what is he doing in the Yiddish theater!"[48]

The "missionary" accusation was to return again and again during Gordin's career, a reference to his earlier life (see discussion below in "Jacob Gordin's Life"). But Goldfaden was no longer a power in the Yiddish theater. There were new forces at work, and Gordin was the leading figure in that change. The *Daytshmerish* gradually disappeared, and the appetite of the audience for the "problem" plays that Gordin had introduced grew. Realism, a literary movement that was dominant in Europe, was being imported into the Yiddish theater, just as Gordin had hoped. But it no longer had to depend on the literal translation of European plays. A new generation began writing in the simple language and on the direct issues that absorbed the immigrant generation.

It was not until his third play, *The Jewish King Lear,* that Gordin finally had a success. In this play he created an absorbing drama, with music; as modified by Jacob Adler, it became one of the great events of the Yiddish stage. It remained in Adler's repertory until his death in 1926. Because of its success, *Lear* was a turning point not only for Gordin, but also for the Yiddish theater. The triumph of realism, however, of a more natural style of speech and acting, was brief. Gordin's death in 1909 coincided with the end of that first tumultuous epoch of the Yiddish theater in America. Within the next decade, the new immigrants were no longer so new; their tastes moved on from anguish and anxiety to nostalgia, and an easier, less fraught atmosphere prevailed. They were no longer riveted by problem dramas. They wanted, instead, the fablelike sweetness of *Green Fields,* wherein a yeshiva student learns to appreciate the virtues of the country and the naïve country girl learns to read and write; they wanted the charming nostalgia of Molly Picon; they wanted the new theater music that owed as much to Tin Pan Alley as to the klezmers. This new tone changed the character of Jewish theater, moving it from an intense emotional experience to an evening of entertainment. The revolution that Gordin had brought to the Yiddish theater did not long outlast him, but a few of his plays remained as classics that were played as long as there was an audience to support a Yiddish speaking company.

Jacob Gordin's Life

Jacob Gordin was one of that generation of Russian Jewish intellectuals passionately committed to rooting out the injustices of Russian society and to eliminating the tsar. Despite their passion, most were fated to emigrate to the United States as the raging violence of the pogroms of 1881 drove them from their homeland. Once there, uprooted from the country that had nurtured their passions, they turned to the new causes and new issues of the New World. Marginalized at home by their Jewishness, and in America by their foreignness, with languages and educations that did not fit into the American mainstream, many of them, to their surprise, found themselves in the world of Jewish culture and letters, an area they had ignored, if not rejected, at home. In New York, their education and secular viewpoint made them natural leaders of the ever-growing immigrant Jewish community, but to reach this public the intellectuals would have to give up their beloved Russian. Russian was a second, a foreign language to the ordinary Jewish immigrant. The newcomers were at home only in Yiddish, and for news and entertainment they read the Yiddish newspapers, which in those days covered every religious and political orientation.

In Russia, Gordin had been born in a time of political ferment, when political movements were led by the young and wellborn, and their issues were discussed endlessly by the intelligentsia in political journals. The emancipation of the serfs in 1861 by Tsar Alexander II, which was meant to solve a long festering problem, seemed only to inflame passions further. The serfs continued to find themselves in a deplorable condition; newly landless, they streamed into the cities, adding to the existing impoverished proletariat. University students in particular made up the backbone of the generation that wanted change in Russia and were deeply involved in the movement called the People's Will (*Narodnaia volia*) — the movement that was responsible for the assassination of the tsar in March 1881. Not all the groups agitating for change were so violent. At the other end of the spectrum were the followers of the great Russian writer Leo Tolstoy, idealists who embraced his theories extolling the virtues of the simple peasant life and led some intellectuals to abandon their pens for the plow. Political theorists added other nuances to the situation, with a growing movement advocating the establishment of a constitutional monarchy. These were all movements that the government felt needed close watching.

Jacob Gordin was born in 1853 in Mirgorod, a town in what is now Ukraine. Gordin's father, a merchant like so many Jews, was a man of the Enlightenment, a Maskil, who still maintained some of his old Hasidic traditions. But when it came to his son's education, he kept him from the conventional Heder, the elementary school for Jewish boys. Instead he had him tutored at home, where he studied Hebrew, Russian, and German. Although Gordin spoke Yiddish as a child, in accordance with his father's wishes the family abandoned Yiddish for Russian. When he came to America, he was reluctant to speak Yiddish, although he wrote it in a perfectly fluent, colloquial style. Bessie Thomashefsky claimed that he spoke like a *goy* [Gentile], pronouncing Yiddish words with a hard Russian "h."[1] Yet he wrote an immense amount in Yiddish. In addition to his eighty full-length plays, he published a volume of one-act plays and four volumes of criticism, travel accounts, New York vignettes, and other essays. This does not take into account his many newspaper articles and lectures, also in Yiddish.

Although his native Mirgorod was small, with unpaved streets, it was prettily located on the Khorol River, and his family was prosperous enough to keep a maid-of-all-work. It was from her, in fact, that Gordin learned Ukrainian. Unlike other immigrants, who could only remember deprivation and squalor, Gordin never lost his nostalgia for the landscape of his homeland. Gordin was a cultivated man, but he had had an unsystematic education. As a naturally voracious reader he filled in some of the gaps, so that he was as familiar with European literature as he was with Russian. But he had no formal training for a profession, no university degree, nothing to prepare him for a particular place in the world. By the age of seventeen he had drifted into journalism, like many young men of his time, writing feuilletons for various Russian periodicals. He seemed to be destined, like so many Jews, to be a *luftmensh* — one who lived by his wits from day to day. Perhaps it was this situation that led him to acquiesce at the age of nineteen to an arranged marriage negotiated by his father with a prosperous family in Elizavetgrad, a city of forty thousand inhabitants, quite large when compared to his tiny home village. His intended bride, Anna, was thirteen years old, at that time not an unusually young age to be betrothed. The girl had no secular education and only the rudimentary learning in Yiddish that was thought sufficient for girls. At some time she must have learned Russian because Gordin's letters to her later in life were written in Russian. Although Gordin went along with all the conventional arrangements made by the families, including moving into his in-laws' house, he insisted that the bride keep her beautiful long hair instead of having it shaved off, as was customary. In addition to a wife, the marriage brought him a substantial dowry, which was supposed to start him on his way to becoming a merchant. But as it turned out, Gordin was a poor businessman and soon lost the dowry in various failed undertakings. Needing money to support his wife and his first child, born a year after his marriage, he entered into a strange period of wandering and trying out one occupation after another. For a while he joined a troupe of traveling players, then he worked on the land as a day laborer, then in ports loading and unloading ships, and finally came to St. Petersburg, where he became a columnist for the Russian newspaper *Nedelya* (The Weekly) writing vignettes about Jewish life. By this time his ideas had matured, so that he wrote not only about what was actually happening, but also his views on how Jews ought to live.[2]

After Gordin returned to Elizavetgrad, he found two groups that appealed to his newly developed sense of the way the world should work. One, the *Stundists,* was essentially an illegal, dissident religious group that had broken away from the Orthodox Church and was therefore regarded with suspicion by the government. It was against religious ceremonies, against icons, against the Sacraments, against drunkenness and smoking — and for a brotherhood of man, for the simple life wherein one lived off one's own work and no one had too much or too little. The *Stundists* were against trade and against the use of money, believing rather in a system of barter. In sum, they believed in one Father in heaven and in one Mother, the earth that produces everything.[3] These ideas were attractive to Gordin, who had been developing his own thoughts about the reform of Judaism. For him, as for the *Stundists,* reform meant simplification. His idea for the reform of Judaism began with nothing less than the elimination of the authority of the Talmud and all the later commentaries that were the basis for Jewish law and a return to the text of the Bible as the sole authority. He wanted to abandon circumcision and also the conventional marriage ceremony. In its place he wanted the couple to appear in the synagogue carrying red flowers as a sign of their union. Like the *Stundists,* he abhorred trade and thought that the Jews should abandon their way of life in Russia, a life heavily based on commerce, and return to the cultivation of the earth. Here, of course, Gordin was beginning to lose sight of reality in his Tolstoyan-*Stundist* haze. He was forgetting that the Jewish occupational structure in Russia was entirely based on the prohibitions that prevented Jews from entering large parts of the working world. They had to make do with the crevices that remained and eke out a living in the most marginal of occupations. They were not permitted to own land. They could enter the professions or government employment only under limited circumstances; the numbers who could enter the universities were restricted, and they were absolutely denied the right to advance in the university system unless they converted. Gordin, in his call to the Jews to abandon trade and cultivate the land, seemed oblivious to the legal restrictions that had pushed them into the corners of the economy in which they found themselves.

A second group that attracted Gordin was founded in Elizavetgrad in January of 1880 by a non-Jew, a Dr. Michailovitch, and was called the Spiritual Biblical Brotherhood; it espoused rather vague principles of nonsectarian brotherhood that exactly suited Gordin's way of thinking. Gordin joined it with great enthusiasm, eventually becoming its principal leader. The nature of this group remains mysterious since reports of people who actually attended the meetings on Saturday afternoons seem to indicate that it had strong religious leanings. After Gordin came to America, however, he gave a lecture which was reported in the Yiddish newspaper *Varhayt* (Truth) denying the brotherhood's religious purpose, saying that religion was merely a pretense, intended to hide from the tsarist police that it was actually a political group.[4] However, its strange religious ideas continued to haunt Gordin in America, where opponents denounced him as a "missionary" attempting to convert Jews to Christianity, citing his participation in the group. The nub of truth behind these recurring accusations was that a disciple of Gordin's, Jacob Priluker, had gone off to Odessa, where he had founded a group called New Israel. And this group, together with Priluker, had indeed converted to Christianity.[5]

But the life of the Spiritual Biblical Brotherhood was abruptly suspended in April 1881. The wave of pogroms that spread over Russia following the assassination of Tsar Alexander II in the preceding month started in Elizavetgrad on April 15 and lasted for three days. Gordin and his wife and four children were sheltered by a gentile neighbor and emerged unscathed, but one hundred Jewish houses in the city had been plundered, one Jew was killed, two hundred were wounded, and the rapes were many and uncounted.[6]

For many Jews this was a turning point, particularly for the young intellectuals who had been drawn to the *Narodnaia* movement, believing that they, as Jews, had a common cause with the peasants against the tyranny of the tsar. As the pogroms continued, they took counsel with themselves and one another. In a dramatic moment shortly after a pogrom in Kiev a group of these students appeared in the synagogue to repent, at a moment

> when the Jewish quarter of Kieff was filled with groans and its pavements were strewn with the debris of destroyed homes. . . . The rabbi had proclaimed a day of fasting and prayer, and the house of God was crowded with sobbing victims of the recent riots. . . . "Brethren," said the spokesman of the delegation . . . , "we are a committee of Jewish students of the university, sent to clasp hands with you and to mingle our tears with your tears. We are here to say to you, 'We are your brothers; like yourselves, like our fathers!' We have striven to adopt the language and manners of our Christian fellow countrymen; we have brought ourselves up to an ardent love of their literature, of their culture, of their progress. We have tried to persuade ourselves that we are children of Mother Russia. Alas! we have been in error. The terrible events which have called forth this fast and these tears have aroused us from our dream. . . . There is no hope for Israel in Russia. The salvation of the downtrodden people lies in other parts, — in a land beyond the seas, which knows no distinction of race or faith, which is mother to Jew and Gentile alike. . . . In America we shall find rest; the stars and stripes will wave over the true home of our people. To America, brethren! To America!"[7]

Of course, not all the intellectuals followed this course. Some, like Solomon Ansky, who later won fame in the Yiddish theater as the author of *The Dybbuk,* decided to share the life of the most wretched of the workers in the tsarist empire. Between 1889 and 1891 Ansky went to work in the mines, severely compromising his health and losing most of his teeth in a bout of scurvy.[8] It took a long intellectual and emotional journey, however, before he was able to reclaim his Jewish heritage and write his masterpiece, which was first produced a month after his death in 1920. Translated into Russian, Hebrew, and other languages, it has remained an imperishable treasure of Yiddish literature.

Most Jews, however, were not afflicted with the revolutionary torments of the Anskys or the Gordins. They saw clearly that Russia held only poverty and tears for them, and, between 1881 and 1924, committed to their own survival, a third of the Jews in the Russian Empire sought salvation elsewhere. These two and a half million scraped together their last kopecks to leave for the United States; it was the poor rather than the rich who had the most urgent reasons to leave. But there was also a smaller movement to emigrate to Eretz Israel, to the land of their fathers — long before the official founding of the Zionist movement. Whichever course individual families chose, the old dream of a peaceful coexistence between Jews and their countrymen was shattered, as we learn from the testimony of the student who spoke in the Kiev synagogue. But Jacob Gordin remained firmly attached to his ideas about the brotherhood of man, despite the evidence of the pogroms, despite the flood of anti-Semitic articles in the Russian press, and he took surprising action. First, he supported and contributed to a fund for the benefit of the families of those who had taken part in the pogroms and had been arrested by the police for their violence. In addition he took the occasion to write an impassioned article in the Russian newspaper *Yuzhni Krai* (Southern Frontier) a few months after the pogrom. It was titled *An Appeal to the Jewish People* and opens with the words "Brother Jews." He starts with the image of the Jewish people as a patient with a painful tooth. The best remedy is for the dentist to pull out the tooth, root and all. In the same way, writes Gordin, the Jews should tear out by the roots their deeply engrained bad habits. He then goes on to discuss these habits, beginning with a question:

> Why do all elements of Russian society hate you? Is it simply a religious hatred? Or is it our love of money, unquenchable, our stinginess, chasing after ways of earning money, our impudence [*chutzpah*], our fawning style, our slavish and foolish imitation of the puffed up and corrupt Russian aristocracy, our usury, our tavern-keeping, our impulse to trade and all our other failings — all these provoke the Russian people against us. Of

course there are also honorable people among us. But they are lost in the mass of traders who day and night think only of how to make a ruble and who never in their lives have had the slightest interest or need for anything else.

Then, referring to the pogroms, he continues:

It is just these events that give me the right to remind you, Brothers, that right now is the time to tear out the rotten teeth with which you have bitten others, and from which you yourselves have suffered from time to time unbearable pain and suffering. Brothers awake! Start a new life. [Meaning—a new life according to the principles of his Spiritual Biblical Brotherhood.][9]

This "appeal," which in essence blamed the victims, received scathing responses in the Yiddish and Hebrew press and remained an ineradicable stain on Gordin's reputation.

Second Phase of the Brotherhood

Unperturbed by the attacks on him, Gordin continued with his life in Elizavetgrad. He had a job as a teacher in a Russian-Jewish school—that is, a Jewish school which also taught secular subjects in Russian—where he was remembered as a stern but inspiring teacher. Then in 1883, two years after the pogroms, the brotherhood started meeting again in what they called their synagogue, with Gordin as their leader. Every Saturday afternoon he would lecture in Russian on a biblical subject or on European literature to members who consisted of both Jews and non-Jews. In 1887 a Christian millionaire, Sibiriakoff, offered the group a huge parcel of six thousand acres in the province of Stavropol on which they could start the agricultural colony of their dreams. But when Gordin traveled to St. Petersburg to claim the land and complete the formalities, he was turned away without any explanation, and the group remained landless.[10]

Although this strange group aroused government uneasiness on both political and religious grounds, for a long time it was protected by the liberal governor of the province. On his departure, however, matters suddenly turned acute for Gordin, who was warned to get out with his family if he did not want to be sent to Siberia. In July 1891, Gordin left for New York to face an uncertain future in a new country. His wife and nine children moved in with her parents to await the time when he would be able to support them in New York. In the end, it took three years before he could afford to bring over his wife and seven of his children. His twenty-year-old daughter, Liza, was left behind with his seventeen-year-old son, Sema. Sema presented a problem; he was mentally retarded, and the family feared he would not be admitted to the new country. Fortunately, when the pair arrived several years later, Sema successfully passed the immigration formalities, and they were able to join their family.

But whether his family was with him or in Russia, Gordin still needed money for their support, and he had to face the New World more earnestly, it would seem, than in Russia. Still committed to the Tolstoyan ideal of agrarian life, Gordin applied to the Baron de Hirsch Fund for help in creating a collective farm. His fellow would-be farmers were all, Gordin wrote, "young, strong, mentally and morally developed." But none had any relevant experience whatsoever; their skills were entirely urban. The Baron de Hirsch Fund refused its aid, and Gordin was obliged to abandon the fantasy and return to journalism.[11]

In Russia, with a basic teaching job and some journalistic work on the side, he could afford to dream, to moralize, and to live according to his ideals. But in the New World he found a very different population of Jews from those in Russia, whose very being had troubled him. In America the Jews were no longer a population of the jobless, of drifters who had no hope of regular employment, of people, as the folk saying had it, " who starved to death three times a day." What he found in this growing industrial society was a vigorous working population. The Jews were poor, they were factory workers, often in the unholy sweatshops so prevalent at the time. But it was also a period in which they were organizing into unions to fight for better conditions. Above all, there was work, and life was not hopeless. The Jews organized socially as well as economically, founding, village by village, their own self-help organizations designed to give support in times of sickness, unemployment and, of course, to arrange for dignified burials. At their height, there were twenty-five hundred such *landsmanshaftn* societies catering to the social, cultural, and economic needs of their members. This was a lively population deeply committed to religious and political causes and outspoken in their beliefs. In addition to their social organizations, this group of immigrants was bent on catching up with the wide world, which had been no more than a mirage in the narrow confines of the Old Country. They founded cultural organizations dedicated to offering lectures on science, history, philosophy, and art, and they devoured the new translations into Yiddish of the great European writers: Byron, Goethe, Dumas, Heine, Turgenev, and Nicolai Cherni-chevsky.[12] Gordin's dreamy ideas found no resonance here, but the new Yiddish theater lived and flourished in this atmosphere wherein the Jewish characters were always noble and spoke magnificently. As the main diversion of these hard-working immigrants, as many as ten theaters on weekend nights found audiences eager to sample this burgeoning art form.

Gordin had friends and helpers among the Russian intellectuals who had preceded him to New York—but their resources were slender. Philip Krantz, a Russian intellectual who had taught himself Yiddish after he arrived, had become the editor of the Social Democratic *Arbeter Tsaytung* and was able to pay Gordin small sums to write in Yiddish for his paper. This was a new experience for Gordin, who had only written in Russian in his homeland. But obviously his early immersion in Yiddish, a language he had heard everyday around him, lent him enough fluency to start a new career in this long-neglected tongue. Three weeks after his arrival he published an article in the *Arbeter Tsaytung* about the three-day pogrom in Elizavetgrad—a theme he could not give up: it became the subject of the third play he wrote for the Yiddish stage in America.

Then in January 1893 Gordin was offered the editorship of a new weekly Russian language newspaper, *Ruski Novosti* (Russian News). Gordin, needing money, was glad to take on the task, although as it turned out he wrote most of the contents himself, using various pseudonyms to disguise this fact. The newspaper had only a short life and closed down less than a year later in November 1893.[13] By this time, however, two years after his arrival in America, his career in the Yiddish theater was firmly launched. As noted earlier, his first play, *Siberia,* had appeared with Jacob Adler in the lead in November 1891. The following month he offered Adler a second play, *Two Worlds, or The Great Socialist,* which Adler declined to use. Gordin, undeterred, went on and wrote yet another drama on a theme that continued to haunt him. His third play, *The Pogrom in Russia,* was accepted by Boris Thomashefsky, and Gordin himself played the role of a Russian-speaking policemen. For this he received an extra five dollars per performance, a welcome addition to his always meager purse.

Bessie Thomashefsky, her husband's partner in the theater, has described her first impression of Gordin when he came to read his play to the company in the office of the Roumanian Opera House. His first encounter with the manager of the company, Moyshe Finkel, set the tone for the meeting. On Gordin's arrival, Finkel saw that he was carrying only a thin notebook under his arm and asked, "Is that all?" To which Gordin replied coolly, "That's enough." "His appearance," Bessie Thomashefsky writes, "impressed us all. He was tall and thin, with a remarkable, handsome and noble face, deep-set, clever eyes, a fine black beard, neatly combed, a great head with thick, black hair that reached his neck. He wore a large, soft black hat with a wide brim and was dressed in a shabby, but clean and fine suit, carrying a walking stick in his hand."[14] His *Pogrom in Russia* ran for three months—a great success at that time—and established him as a figure to be reckoned with, with his new kind of play, in the Yiddish theater.

The impression of dignity and power Gordin exuded, despite his penurious appearance, is repeated again and again in the memoirs of those who knew him. Leon Kobrin, one of his biographers, describes Gordin's presence in one of his favorite cafés among a group of writers, musicians, community activists, and others: "He impresses them all, it would appear, with his commanding, imposing figure, with his unusually impressive appearance. As he sits there, among them, with his long, pitch-black beard, with his sharp, commanding black eyes, and with his assured and proud demeanor, he reminds one of a prophet from Biblical times in the circle of his students and followers. With how much respect they gaze into his eyes and with what delight they take in his every word! If he takes out a cigar to smoke, there suddenly appear a half dozen hands with lit matches."[15]

Gordin's breakthrough in the Yiddish theater came in 1892, when he signed a contract with Adler to become the playwright for his company. This was no small undertaking since he would have to write four or five plays in a season. His first play under this contract was *The Jewish King Lear.* Although Gordin had begun to build a reputation with his earlier plays, the actors still worried as they saw their usual latitude to improvise, to sing and dance as it suited them, suddenly taken away under Gordin's iron hand. Boaz Young, a new actor in Adler's company, was present at the first reading of the play to the assembled company. It took place in the saloon next to Poole's Theater, which Adler had leased for the season, and it was not a happy event. This time Gordin was not present, and Adler read the manuscript to his company. I am assuming that what he read was the manuscript translated here. Gordin seems to have brought over from Russia a stock of children's school notebooks, and *Lear* was written in just such a little copybook, like the one that had aroused the anxiety of Thomashefsky's manager. If Adler was expecting enthusiasm from his company he didn't get it, and Young reports that they had nothing but complaints and criticism. They did not see room in the tightly constructed play for the improvisations, the skits and songs they were accustomed to inserting. Young wrote, "When Adler finished reading, and the troupe was leaving the saloon, I heard Bernstein joke, 'What will I do in that play? Catch flies? Ha!' Tobachnikoff was beside himself. 'Is this what Adler brought me to America for? I haven't even a spot to sing a number. And what kind of part is that for Adler? Some ordinary old Jew in a long coat and a *yarmulke . . .*'

'It'll be on the boards from Friday to Saturday,' another joked."

Only the prompter had a good word to say about the play: "Yes, children, I see that the play does not please you. But I see that this piece will make a great success. I see also that it will play for a long time. We only need to change the name, but unfortunately the Jew with the black beard won't let us do that."[16]

When *The Jewish King Lear* opened in October 1892 at Poole's Theater, there were two other Yiddish plays running: Boris Thomashefsky at the Thalia Theater in his great hit by Lateiner, *Alexander, the Crown Prince of Jerusalem,* and David Kessler in the equally successful musical by Hurwitz, *The Daughter of the Priest.* Thomashefsky and Kessler appeared in thrill-producing tights and were supported by elaborate stage sets, costumes, music, and lights. Given this new, sober drama, Adler had to hope for a very different audience. He was not disappointed: *The Jewish King Lear* offered them a level of profound satisfaction in the theater they had not known before. Suddenly they saw before them all the old neighbors, all the characters who had been part of their village life in the Old Country. Who didn't remember the old tyrannical rich man who sat in a place of honor at the East Wall of the synagogue and who expected everything to go his way? And Khane Leah, the long-suffering wife who keeps her head in that terrific welter of emotion and greed when Dovidl distributes his fortune. "What about us?" she asks reasonably. "What will we live on?" And the two sons-in-law were also vividly familiar. One knew just what their response would be to every situation: the tight, humorless Misnagid and the easygoing, irresponsible Hasid. One could feel the sigh of comfort as the audience settled into the play. They were home. Adler himself, in his long gabardine and fur hat, aroused a storm of recognition as he entered to take his place at the Purim table. As Sara Adler (Jacob's young wife), who

Jacob P. Adler's Grand Theatre in New York City. The marquee reads "Thur. night: King Lear." (Museum of the City of New York)

played Taybele in the first production, wrote in her memoirs, "I have in my time witnessed ovations for great artists. . . . Adler's Yiddish 'King' seated at the head of his holiday table created such a moment. From the orchestra to the gallery, the theater crashed! His part had 'taken' before he spoke a word. And this was nothing to the scenes that came later! He was not an actor that night, but a force. All of us played with inspiration, but the great figure that night Gordin had given to Adler, and the triumph was his own."[17] As the theater historian B. Gorin has pointed out, the audience could not judge how a king or a prince of two thousand years ago might act, but they were all experts on their neighbors in the *shtetl*.

It is no wonder, as Young reports, that the new immigrants brought their children to see the play. All the complexities and color of their old life that they could never seem to convey to an indifferent American generation were here displayed before them. "Fathers," wrote Young, "took their children to the theater, so that they could absorb the moral of the play. And hundreds of thank-you letters arrived for Adler from Jewish mothers: their Moysheles and Shloymeles had become better people, since they had seen the piece. "[18]

These all seem like extravagant reactions in our more temperate or cynical times. But the Yiddish theater at that moment was exactly the arena in which these unsettled emotions played themselves out — and in even more extravagant forms, as we shall see. There is no doubt that *The Jewish King Lear* was the turning point, not only in Gordin's career, but also in the American Yiddish theater. The play gave legitimacy to the spoken word without the extravagance of song and dance and glitter.

Gordin lived only eighteen years after his night of triumph, but he continued to write at the same furious pace, turning out, predictably, some failures along with his successes. But in this period he discovered three dramatic actresses — Keni Liptzin, Sara Adler, and Bertha Kalish — whose talents so impressed him that he wrote plays especially designed for their particular gifts. One of his imperishable plays, *Mirele Efros: The Jewish Queen Lear,* was written for Keni Liptzin and opened in New York in August 1898. The only relationship the two *Lears* have to one another is that the protagonist in each is powerful, headstrong, and rich. Otherwise the two plots run along very different lines. But as in the earlier *Lear,* once again the sense of recognition of familiar types from the Old Country gave the play an extra force among the audience: the sly daughter-in-law and her grasping mother; the foolish father; the besotted son. All were richly

יאקאב פ. אדלער, אלס דער יודישער קעניג ליער.

Jacob Adler as Lear. (Archives of the YIVO Institute for Jewish Research)

understood characters that gave the audience not only enjoyment but also a sense of command as the play progressed. They *knew* these people!

New Causes in a New Country

Gordin, like the other Russian Jewish intellectuals, soon found that the issues and problems that had beset him at home were no longer relevant. But there was no scarcity of social causes, and Gordin was quick to see them and use them as themes for his new plays. One of his pervasive themes is feminism, the feminism embodied by Taybele in *Lear* at the moment when she declares that she wants to be educated so that she can become a "useful person." In an even more direct statement, in his play *The Wild Man* the daughter of the family makes a memorable speech that condemns the entire system of traditional Jewish education for girls. Her widowed father has decided to bring his new, younger wife into the household, and the wife immediately demands that the daughter leave. The father acquiesces, and the daughter then speaks to the couple about her prospects in life:

> Liza. Have you given any thought to how I will find means to support myself?
>
> Zelda [the stepmother]. You're the clever one, someone who gets things done. You aren't afraid of anything. People like you don't die of hunger.
>
> Liza. Work—it's easy to say "go and work." But for what kind of work have you educated me? Don't think that I've sat and waited until your beloved wife, the highly esteemed Madam Zelda, drove me from your house. It is already three months that I've been going about the city looking for work. When I apply at a bank, they ask me whether I know European languages. No, I have not learned European languages. If I go to the office of a large bakery, they ask me if I know Italian bookkeeping. No, I don't know it. I haven't studied it. In a fashionable department store, they ask me if I am a milliner. But I am my father's child—a girl of good family, the only daughter. I have not studied anything. The seamstress asks me if I can sew or cook or wash or iron. No. In my father's house there were servants. They baked and cooked and ironed. I can't do anything. I never learned. Yes, I want to go and work. But I want to ask you, for what kind of work have you educated me? Now answer me. You are rid of me, but you have no right not to answer this question.
>
> Shmuel [the father]. Such foolishness! I ask you. How do all Jewish daughters grow up? If you had wanted to take care of yourself and be a

normal person, I would have arranged for you to be married, and you would have lived the way all women live. But you are too clever. So do what you understand best . . .

Liza. Yes. All Jewish fathers prepare their daughters only for their weddings. But life is not a wedding. Why don't you prepare us for life? Why do you ruin us with your sort of education? Why do you cripple us and make us into good-for-nothings?[19]

To Gordin's theater audience, filled with young women working in menial jobs in factories, such a speech would have resonated powerfully. If only *they* had been educated, how much better they would be living now, in what fine jobs they would now be working!

The vulnerable position of women in the stratified Jewish world, no less than in the modern American life to which they came, continued to arouse Gordin in play after play. In his *Sappho* he explores the subject of out-of-wedlock pregnancy. In the play, the heroine Sofia is a young working woman who is, in fact, supporting her shiftless father as well as the rest of her family. On the eve of her wedding, knowing she is pregnant by her intended husband, she discovers that he actually loves her sister. In a sweeping gesture, she renounces him and insists that the wedding go forward with her sister as the bride. She goes on to bear her illegitimate child and continues to support her family. The "happy ending" is less important than the ringing speeches Gordin wrote for his heroine. At the turning point of the play, Sofia addresses her intended, revealing her secret on the day before the wedding in a room crowded with friends and relatives:

Yes, the whole world must know that too. I . . . must become a mother. I am not ashamed. I loved the man. And one who loves faithfully must have faith, must believe, must sacrifice everything in the world. Yes, I had faith and sacrifice. That will not force me to marry him when I feel and understand that I must not be his wife. . . . I made a mistake, it is my error and my misfortune. It is nobody's business. I take all the responsibility. Strangers with their piety and righteousness, with their laughter and mockery will not force me to stifle, to bury, the truth and to act against my feelings. If I am to be a mother, I can care for my child by myself. Nothing frightens me. I will be free and honorable in my actions, honorable the way I understand it, not Aunt Frade's way and Uncle Melekh's and all the rest![20]

Other themes that concerned the helplessness of women provided Gordin with the subjects for new plays — some of which aroused strong reactions from the conservative or religious Yiddish press, which saw Gordin as questioning the fundamental principles of Jewish family life. His play *The Slaughter* (the title in Yiddish is *Di Shehita*, a word reserved for ritual kosher slaughter by a trained expert) takes up in a grisly way the long-vexed question of the arranged marriage. Here Gordin depicts a young girl in love with a poor young man who is studying to be a ritual slaughterer. Without regard for her feelings, her parents push her into a marriage with a rich old man, since this alliance will rescue them from poverty. The old man is a brute who humiliates his new wife by ostentatiously flaunting his mistress, his children's governess, in his house.

Suffering and despairing, this simple girl begins to break down. When she is suddenly awakened one night by noises from her husband's room, she seizes a knife, actually the ritual knife of her former love, who has visited her that day and accidentally left it behind. And with that she murders her husband. This was the most violent illustration possible of the evil consequences of an old institution, but Gordin did not shrink from extravagant action when he wanted to make his point.

A less widespread problem but nonetheless agonizing for those caught in its toils was that posed by the strict laws surrounding the *agunah,* or "the chained wife." A woman whose husband disappeared was left without the recourse of divorce since, according to Jewish law, it is the husband who must initiate and grant the divorce. In the early years of Jewish mass immigration to this country, many men deserted their families; the *Forward,* in fact, ran a kind of rogue's gallery for a while with the pictures of these missing men. But the abandoned women lived the rest of their lives in limbo. Even in Europe, this was an important issue for the Maskilim, who strongly criticized the rigidity of the rabbinic courts that deprived thousands of women of the right to full lives with love, children, and families.

Gordin took up this theme in his play *The Stranger,* inspired by Alfred, Lord Tennyson's "Enoch Arden" but giving it a turn that Tennyson could not have imagined. Tennyson's wildly popular poem of 1864 tells the tragic tale of a poor fisherman who goes off to sea to support his wife and children. Shipwrecked on a deserted Eden, Enoch endures years of solitude before he is rescued. He returns home, gray with age, to find that his wife had waited loyally for him for eleven years and then, convinced of his death, had married again. She and her children are enjoying a happy, prosperous life with the second husband. Nobly, Enoch Arden refrains from revealing his identity until he is close to death, when he tells his story to a sympathetic friend who conveys his dying blessing to his wife and children and to the man who has taken his place.

In Gordin's play, a shopkeeper's son-in-law resists an attempted robbery of the store and kills one of the thieves. He is condemned to an indeterminate term in Siberia and is sent away. After many years pass without word from him, his wife, Blume, presumes him dead and marries his best friend. They move to New York with their children, a daughter by her first marriage and a son by her second. After a while, they are visited by a "stranger" from their hometown who is, of course, the long-lost husband. For the stranger's entertainment, the daughter recites a poem she has learned for school. This is the pure Gordin touch, for the poem is none other than "Enoch Arden." The play turned out to be very popular, although it was not one of Gordin's favorites; he is reported to have reproached his audience in one of his curtain speeches for preferring it to one of his more difficult plays.[21] Nonetheless, it was one of Jacob Adler's most popular roles, and he played it to great effect throughout his stage career.

One of Gordin's most successful plays was *The Kreutzer Sonata* written for one of his favorite actresses, Bertha Kalish. It opened in 1902 to great acclaim and in the following year was translated into English and performed in Chicago with the American actress Blanche Walsh in the lead role. In this play, we find Gordin in a doubly didactic mood. In his choice of title we see his usual wish to educate the unschooled, nonwesternized immigrant audience, an audience who generally had no idea who Tolstoy was and no clue about Beethoven and his Kreutzer Sonata. In the very first scene, the heroine, Eti, enters her parents' drawing room carrying a book. When her father asks her about it, she says it is *The Kreutzer Sonata,* and she immediately tells the Tolstoy story, also explaining the meaning of the title.

Despite the identical titles, the two works have little in common. The Tolstoy story is narrated by a jealous husband and is vintage late Tolstoy in attacking the mores of conventional society. The husband rants about the dishonesty and hypocrisy of Russian upper-class customs and concludes that there can be no love in marriage since each partner is intent on exploiting the other for his or her selfish motives.

The husband receives a shock when he introduces into his household a young man, a violinist who immediately proposes that he and the wife, who is an excellent pianist, play some duets together. The husband at first

Kalish, one of Gordin's favorite actresses, for whom he wrote *The Kreutzer Sonata*. (Archives of the YIVO Institute for Jewish Research)

accepts this new entertainment until he begins to notice the deep, almost sexual satisfaction that these duets, particularly the Kreutzer Sonata, give his wife. Although the reader is never given the faintest suggestion that the duets led to any illicit encounters, the husband grows more and more convinced that his wife is betraying him. Returning unexpectedly from a trip one evening, he discovers his wife and the violinist having an intimate supper together. He goes to his study, takes an ornamental dagger off the wall, and confronts the two in a towering rage. The violinist simply runs out of the room and out of the house. Left alone with his wife, the husband stabs her with his dagger.

In Gordin's play, there are a few formal similarities to Tolstoy's tale, but Gordin's message is totally different. We discover at the beginning of the play that Eti is pregnant by a Russian officer. The two had wanted to marry; Eti was even willing to convert from Judaism to Christianity, but the officer's parents are dead-set against the marriage and forbid their son to proceed. In despair, he commits suicide, never knowing of Eti's condition.

To rescue her honor, her father, a rich merchant, manages to buy a young, ambitious violinist who is eager to go to America to further his career and will marry Eti as a way of getting there. He explains the obstacles to his career in Russia. Although he was offered a position by the St. Petersburg Philharmonic Orchestra, it was on the condition that he abandon Judaism and convert. The offer by Eti's father to buy them ship tickets to America, plus a handsome dowry and five hundred rubles travel money, seems like an answer to his dream. When he is left alone with Eti, she tells him that she is pregnant and also tells him the name of the father. He accepts the news with good grace, and arrangements are made for the wedding.

Meanwhile we have been treated to Eti's sister, Tsili, playing the piano in great style. The violinist is attracted to her playing and suggests that they play the Kreutzer Sonata together. The audience, which has just been told the plot of Tolstoy's story, is now prepared for a catastrophe.

But Gordin surprises them; the plot goes off in an entirely different direction. Life in America is not easy for Eti. Her husband, Gregoire, hates her son, and when he gives the child his violin lessons he reproaches him for every mistake with the epithet "Officer's son!" After a few years, Tsili and the rest of the family emigrate to America to be close to Eti, her father's favorite child. Meanwhile Gregoire is revealed as a tyrannical husband intent on humiliating Eti at every point, criticizing her both with and without reason and commanding her to do his bidding without question. Then, in a puzzling turn of events, we see him from time to time behaving tenderly toward her and declaring his love.

Meanwhile, Tsili comes and goes freely in the household and continues to play duets with Gregoire. At the climax of the play, when Tsili confesses that she has had a child by Gregoire but has given it away, Gregoire announces that he and Tsili are going to the opera that evening and commands Eti not to stir from the house and await his return. Eti's brother arrives shortly after their departure and says that he too had planned to go to the opera that evening to hear *Carmen*. Since the prima donna was suddenly indisposed, the opera was canceled. As *The Meistersinger* was to be presented instead, he decided to come home.

When Tsili and Gregoire return later in the evening, they are full of enthusiasm for the prima donna and Tsili even sings one of her arias from *Carmen*. Eti finally exposes their lie and makes a passionate speech about Gregoire's brutal treatment of her. Her main point is that he feels he has complete rights over her body, that he can require sexual gratification whenever he wants it, while he is under no obligation to treat her humanely between these episodes. Finally, maddened by Tsili's taunts picturing her as an innocent fool and by her own fury at ten years of humiliation at Gregoire's hands, Eti picks up a revolver left by her father on the piano and shoots them both dead.

Except in its use of the Kreutzer Sonata as a symbol of intimacy and the violent ending, Gordin's play has only the most superficial resemblance to Tolstoy's story; it is most original in its exposure of the arbitrary sexual relations that existed not only in conventional Jewish society, wherein the husband exercised unlimited authority over his wife, but also in Victorian society at large. Gordin's boldness in presenting a taboo subject must have accounted for the play's popular success. It was particularly relevant to his audience of young immigrants questioning the old ways in the new freedom of America. For the young women especially, who had achieved spectacular independence as self-supporting working women, the old rules were no longer acceptable. Their rights didn't stop in the workplace, and marriage in America was to change the old master-servant relationship forever.

The play that really aroused the ire of the Orthodox Jews in New York was Gordin's *Hasia, the Orphan*. This play also exposed a problem, well

known not only in Jewish households but also in well-to-do homes every-
where, in which young, inexperienced servant girls were often taken ad-
vantage of by the men of the house and then dismissed in disgrace when
they became pregnant. Sholem Aleichem chose just this theme to start his
one-act play *Mentshn* (domestics). When the servant Liza is fired because
she is pregnant by the master of the house, the cook urges her to take
a job at some distance from their town and "provide yourself with a
dowry . . . to have a household of your own, little fool, and keep your own
mentshn."[22] Gordin's way of presenting the problem is hardly as genial.
The heroine of *Hasia, the Orphan* is a naïve girl who has grown up in a
little village. When her mother dies, she is sent by her father to live as a
servant in her uncle's house in a big city. In this play she is molested not
only by the master of the house, her uncle, but also by his son, Vladimir,
and even by the son-in-law to be. Vladimir eventually seduces Hasia and
then makes up for it by marrying her. But this hardly ends the matter. The
son turns out to be a wastrel and a drunkard who neglects his wife when he
is not mistreating her. In despair she is driven to take poison and commit
suicide.

This play was a box office hit but aroused a violent attack from the
conservative *Tageblat,* which accused Gordin of impugning the purity of
the Jewish family and was outraged that young people should be exposed
to such immoral behavior. But the young women in the audience were not
the sheltered daughters of the bourgeoisie. These were young women
working in the shops, women who everyday saw coercive foremen attempting to win sexual favors from unprotected girls or were forced to
hear the lewd language of fellow workers intent on embarrassing them.
The young women in the audience understood Gordin better than the
editors of the *Tageblat,* who were not daily confronting the realities of the
workplace.

Not content with attacking the play, the *Tageblat* went on to attack
Gordin personally. The editors claimed that he had headed an organiza-
tion in Russia whose purpose was the conversion of the Jews. And not
only that, but his perfidy continued into the present. He was now involved
with the anarchists, they claimed, in a plot to take over the Yiddish stage,
to make it the instrument for spreading anarchist ideas in order to destroy
Jewish family life. Although these accusations were countered with passionate letters to the *Forward* by supporters of Gordin, the matter did not
end with letters. In October 1903, shortly after the review appeared, the

Socialists convened a mass protest meeting in New York, and a week later Gordin himself stepped before the curtains at a performance of the play to denounce the review in the *Tageblat*.[23]

But Gordin did not always choose the most popular side in controversies. In *The Russian Jew in America,* a play about unionization, Gordin showed himself to be out of touch with his public. His nostalgia for Russia was not theirs. They saw themselves getting ahead in America and would not have returned to the Old Country for the world. In their new lives, the unions gave them power in their struggle to rein in the greed of the sweatshop bosses and win a better life for themselves. Gordin, in his contrarian mode, chose to show the union chief in his play as a man who is corrupt and stupid. This so outraged Abe Cahan, editor of the pro-union Socialist newspaper, *Arbeter Tsaytung,* that he stood up in the middle of the first performance shouting (in Russian), "It's a lie" and stamped out of the theater.[24]

Although Gordin lived for eighteen years in the United States, it was not until the last years of his life that he applied for and obtained American citizenship. Until then he had been thoroughly wrapped in his cocoon of the Russian intellectual in exile longing for the fields and forests of his homeland. He had also brought with him the European intellectual's endemic contempt for the crude and brash life of America, contempt for its lack of culture. This very comforting prejudice has persisted in generations of Europeans whose ideas were formed before they ever set foot on American soil. And many, like Gordin, never got to know the real America. Gordin, as was well known, spent his evenings in Zeitlin's Café drinking tea with his fellow Russian intellectuals and Yiddish actors. As long as he set his plays in the Old Country his characters, however extravagant their behavior, all bore the convincing stamp of truth. When he wrote about America it was the didactic strain, rather than heartfelt realism, that moved the play along. In his *Russian Jew in America,* the play that so roused Abe Cahan to fury, Gordin was writing about unions in a way that made no sense to his audience. In the embryonic unions of the period, the corruption of union leaders was a nonissue. The real enemies were the bosses and their starvation wages and, even worse, the thugs hired by the bosses whenever a strike was called. These hooligans did not hesitate to break a few heads in their attempt to intimidate the defenseless strikers. One of the most popular songs of the period, "Motl der Aprayter" (Motl the Operator), is about a poor garment worker who joins his union's

strike and is clubbed to death by the hired thugs of the bosses. This was the
real workers' issue. Gordin was off the point.

Similarly, Gordin's play about the hopelessness of intermarriage, *The
Truth,* begins with a rowdy group of boys throwing stones at an old Jew
arriving at his daughter's house. The group is led by the man's own grand-
son, a boy who has never known of his Jewish heritage. For Gordin this
incident has all the horror of a pogrom — part of an everlasting, ineradicable pattern. But again, this was not how such attacks were perceived in
America, where pogroms were unknown and the occasional occurrences
of street rowdyism were taken for what they were: isolated incidents. The
random act of a gang of boys did not convey even to newly arrived American Jews the deep-rooted, eternally recurrent pogroms of Russia. For once
Gordin's realism portrayed less than he imagined, since his contact with
real Americans was almost nonexistent.

In his choice of intermarriage as a theme, Gordin had again missed the
mark. The immigrant generation was hardly afflicted with the problem of
intermarriage. For them intermarriage meant the marriage of an immigrant with an Americanized Jew. Marriage with a non-Jew was not even
thinkable. Deeply rooted in the old culture and entirely Yiddish-speaking,
the young newcomers socialized with others like themselves; they lived,
worked, and shopped entirely in their own community and married within
it as well. Gordin's anguished approach stood in stark contrast to the far
more easygoing approach taken by the popular farce *Abie's Irish Rose,*
written for the American stage by Anne Nichols in 1922. *Abie's Irish Rose*
took a lighthearted, convivial view of intermarriage; the initial parental
opposition on both sides gives way to an ending that promises happiness
and family approval of the young couple. The play ran successfully on
Broadway for five years. It represented a hopeful approach to a problem
that surely cost heartache, as the first American-born generation began to
cross the old ethnic lines. But in Gordin's generation it hardly existed.

In several ways, *The Truth* was an anomaly in Gordin's work. As one of
his more astute biographers, Zalman Zilbercweig, points out, for the first
time in a life dedicated to the brotherhood of man Gordin chooses to
show how impossible it is.[25] There was a difficulty with the language too.
To emphasize the unbridgeable differences between the Jews in his play
and the non-Jews, the non-Jews as well as the Americanized Jews speak in a
dry, stilted way. By contrast the ordinary Jew speaks a rich, full Yiddish
embroidered with sayings and proverbs that ornament every sentence. On

the surface, then, it appears to be a homage to Yiddish, a redeeming feature in a play otherwise wooden and mechanical.

What has happened to the old internationalist Gordin, Zilbercweig worries? But he didn't have long to wait. Two years later, in 1905, Gordin engaged in a public debate with Chaim Zhitlowsky, a well-known Jewish nationalist and a passionate advocate of Yiddish as the national language as opposed to Hebrew, the language advocated by the Zionists.

In the debate the old dreamer Gordin was back. "Today," he said, "we have only two kinds of nations, the humane and the inhumane, the exploited and the exploiters, those who are productive and those who wait idly to be fed. That struggle now goes on between these two nations will sooner or later lead to a conclusion in which there will be only one people, one kingdom, one culture, one civilization, one great union which will call itself by the great, holy name: Humanity."[26]

Against Zhitlowsky's creed that Yiddish was a language that formed a special national Yiddish culture, that it would "unite Jews in a single grand nation," Gordin saw Yiddish as only the first step for the Jews toward acquiring other languages and becoming cosmopolitan. Although this creed reflected perhaps Gordin's own strivings, the reality was that he could and did write a rich, full Yiddish deeply embedded in a complex folk culture. However much he may have looked down on the "Jargon" in which he wrote his plays, he used it to powerful effect as someone who was, despite himself, deeply connected to the language and culture.

Gordin's attachment was not only to his old ideas, but also to the habits he had formed in his early years. Even his loyal friend Morris Winchevsky could not help noticing Gordin's unbending faithfulness to the habits of the Old Country. Winchevsky cites three examples. Gordin never gave up the old habit of drinking his tea through a sugar cube held between his teeth. And although others in his group had long abandoned their canes, Gordin carried his. And finally, Winchevsky mentions Gordin's dramatic long black beard — an adornment the others gave up on their arrival in America.[27]

But Gordin's last trip to Europe in 1907–08 seems to have led to a change of heart. By this time the cancer of the esophagus that would eventually kill him had begun to show itself, and Gordin, in good European fashion, traveled to Carlsbad to take the waters. The trip was also designed for him to visit the various Yiddish theater groups in eastern Europe, particularly the company performing in Lemberg under the direction of

Jacob Gordin in his fifties, with a long white beard, still wearing his old-fashioned Russian hat and coat. (Archives of the YIVO Institute for Jewish Research)

Max Gimpel. As Gordin discovered, 95 percent of the plays they presented were of American origin. And his own work, with its simplicity and lack of elaborate stage effects, was particularly appealing to a company with no resources. Zilbercweig quotes from Gordin's description of what he saw:

"Herr Gimpel's theater," writes Gordin, "in the capital of Galicia, is as similar to a theater as a turkey is to a hot air balloon. A courtyard, surrounded by a wooden fence. In the middle of the courtyard a mountain of garbage, a few drooping trees, a few broken wooden benches, a stage knocked together with boards. Here is where they play in the summer. In the winter they play in a stable in the same courtyard. Thousands of people throng together to see a piece while sitting crowded together, in the narrowest space, and choking on the various smells in the stable. If one wants to show a forest, or a mountain, a temple or a ship, a poor house or a princely palace, one and the same backdrop fulfills all these functions with a few smeared trees. As for their costumes or technical equipment! If one needs to drink wine, the actor pretends to pour wine from an empty bottle and pretends to drink. . . . The first time I was at the theater, the company played my *Wild Man*. Or at least that was what it had announced on the posters. I barely held out until the last act. Help! You should have seen what a mess they made of my poor play. At the end, I thanked the public for their warm reception, but I had to tell them that at least seventy-five percent of the play that they had seen was not by me. The audience, the actors and the Herr Director were all astonished by my undiplomatic remarks."[28]

Gordin here must be referring to a fifth act that was tacked on to the play to create a happy ending instead of the grisly murder that concludes Gordin's play. But the director was dissatisfied not only with Gordin's remarks, but also with the fact that he didn't speak German. What he didn't know, as Gordin writes, is that

for sixteen years I have fought a little battle in America against *Daytshmerish*, [that strange Germanic corruption of Yiddish that had become a permanent feature of the Yiddish stage] and it has finally been driven from the Yiddish theater in America. I hope that the next time I come to Galicia, the Yiddish theater will not be less Yiddish-speaking than the theater in America. I went home sadly from the 'theater' and thought — what a fine audience, with such intelligent faces capable of so much genuine enthusiasm with such a passionate desire to see good plays and there is no theater for them. In Russia, they still don't have a clue as to what the Yiddish theater is. There it's just on the level with Purim plays. . . . In both countries, they produce plays and feed the public with the same low-class trash [*shund*]. And if once in a while they produce a better play, it's

shamefully murdered and crippled. The Russian critics write condescend-
ingly about America. However poor the Yiddish theater may be in America, whatever mistakes they make — they deserve respect! Hats off, you
who are drowning in trash and in rags, when you speak of Yiddish drama
and Yiddish theater in America![29]

In 1911, two years after Gordin's death, the Lemberg troupe traveled
to Prague to perform for several weeks at the Café Savoy. Again, this was
not a real theater, and the actors performed on a little stage while café life
continued to go on. Nonetheless the unique experience of hearing Yiddish
plays drew many theatergoers, among them Franz Kafka. Kafka knew no
Yiddish but claimed that anyone who spoke German could understand
Yiddish. In this case, of course, the Gimpel troupe was meeting their
audience halfway because of its use of Daytshmerish. Kafka was fascinated
by the prima donna in the company and also developed a strong friendship with the leading actor in the company, Itzak Lowy. Lowy's greatest
performance was in the title role of Gordin's *Wild Man*; the "wild man" is
in fact a boy, a young, retarded, horrifyingly disturbed youth who forms a
terrible passion for his stepmother and in the climactic final scene consum-
mates his desire by murdering her. And Kafka attended every performance
over a period of three weeks. This has led some scholars to speculate that
Gordin's play was the inspiration for Kafka's *Metamorphosis*.[30] Although
the plot is different, Kafka's story echoes the central narrative of Gordin's
more complex storyline: like Gordin, Kafka tells a story of a family over-
come by shame at their aberrant child. Kafka's story opens with the hero,
Gregor Samsa, the son of a comfortable Czech family, waking in his bed
one morning to discover that during the night he has been transformed
into a giant cockroach. His parents react with horror and do their best to
hide him away in their apartment. This parallels the treatment of the
defective son in Gordin's play, who is also kept hidden by his family. The
second parallel element is that in each play there is one sibling who does
not forget the humanity of these problematic creatures and attempts to
show some sympathy.

Gordin's health did not improve after his return home, but it was not
until November of 1908 that his condition was finally accurately diag-
nosed. Cancer of the esophagus was untreatable, and, after many hospital
stays, he was finally sent home to die. The best his doctors could do for
him was to give him some morphine to control his pain.

Nonetheless, in the last year of his life Gordin wrote another play — on an American topic. It was called *Dementia America* and dealt with a recent real estate scandal in which many poor Jews had lost money. Gordin personalized this story by making his protagonist a Russian intellectual who comes to America and is corrupted by the American pursuit of riches. His early efforts to earn an honest living are derailed when the café he runs is taken over by gamblers, who teach him the quick and dirty tricks of making easy money. He becomes a speculator and goes deep into debt to buy some apartment houses in the Bronx, Brownsville, and Washington Heights. He manages to get two mortgages to finance this scheme and for a while his family enjoys the high life, his wife laden with diamonds. But when the bank holding his mortgages suddenly goes bankrupt he is left with nothing but the huge debts he has incurred in his real estate maneuvers.

Both Jacob Adler and David Kessler optioned the play in turn, but in the end chose safer fare and gave up on it. Boris Thomashefsky, however, decided that the role was for him and opened it in November 1908. It turned out to be a sensational success with audiences and critics alike. Even Cahan, who had been writing biting criticism of Gordin in his *Forward*, relented and magnanimously compared the play to Henrik Ibsen's *Master Builder*. Then after two weeks of success, Thomashefsky suddenly closed the play. Many years later he confessed he had done so under pressure from New York real estate interests.[31]

On May 1, 1909, Gordin's friends gathered at his house in Brooklyn to celebrate his fifty-sixth birthday. This was the sort of occasion and company that Gordin could enjoy intensely. By then, however, his disease had begun to attack him in ways that could no longer be denied. He had lost forty pounds and was having increasing difficulty swallowing. By the next day, he could no longer leave his bed. At this point, he and his family lived in a certain comfort in the roomy house in Brooklyn he had bought and renovated. Its main center was his book-lined study on the second floor, where he received his friends and socialized. But even that became too difficult, and his family found it necessary to hire full-time nursing care in order to keep him comfortable.

Winchevsky, his closest friend, lived in an agony of grief and helplessness as he watched his friend deteriorate. In a little book entitled *A Day with Jacob Gordin*, Winchevsky describes actually a day in his own life which is entirely given over to thinking about Gordin, his work, and his accomplishments. It concludes with his last visit on June 10, 1909. He arrived at the house to find he was the only friend in the parlor downstairs, where the family was assembled. Around 9:15 in the evening the nurse came downstairs to summon him to Gordin's room:

> As this was the first time in ten days that he had expressed such a wish, it was with something like fear I went upstairs to see him. He looked much better than I expected because during the day we had heard terrible bulletins from the sick room. I went in and took his hand in mine and looked at him very closely, expecting to hear that 'song without words' that his slowly departing great spirit had sung in the last days. I awaited one of those quiet silent scenes to which we had all become accustomed.
>
> Suddenly I heard his voice. It was not a whisper, as he had spoken ever since he had come back from the hospital, not half-choked, as a week earlier, when it seemed as if his voice were already coming out of the grave. But clear and almost loud, he made himself heard. He said, "Winchevsky, *finita la commedia!*"
>
> It was so loud and clear that everyone in the room could hear the words. Jacob Gordin's last words.
>
> An hour later, he was hardly aware of anything around him. By half past eleven he was unconscious. By a quarter after twelve, he had died. Then his great spirit took leave of his body and the art of the Yiddish theater as well.[32]

At his funeral, two hundred fifty thousand New Yorkers turned out to pay their respects, and of these ten thousand accompanied the family to the cemetery.

As was very soon evident, however, Gordin's death and his absence as a force in the theater were a terrible loss to the kind of serious drama he had single-handedly brought to the Yiddish theater. By December 1909, only a half year after Gordin's death, Keni Liptzin in an interview with the *Forward* was blaming "the resurgence of *shund* on the post-Gordin dramatists, the managers who are afraid of literary drama and, of course, the press."[33] For her the Gordin epoch was over!

Not until the arrival of Maurice Schwartz and his Yiddish Art Theater in 1918 did the Yiddish stage finally find an arena and a company for the fine work coming out of Poland from the pens of the Singer brothers, for Ansky's *The Dybbuk,* and for occasional revivals of Gordin's plays.

None of Gordin's children followed him into either Yiddish literature or the Yiddish theater. His son Alexander did make occasional translations of Gordin plays and wrote an introduction to a collection of Gordin's one-act plays wherein he denounced the commercial Yiddish theater in very strong language. We can only presume it was in retaliation for the hardship suffered by his family as his father slowly made his way in that jungle, haggling year in and year out with stingy managers. Alexander wrote his contribution in English, but it was translated into Yiddish for publication.[34]

Our last view of Anna is with Alexander, who was a chess prodigy and made his living by running a chess parlor on 42nd Street in Manhattan over a penny arcade. There, a Yiddish writer named Leon Kustan, who was a chess enthusiast, came to know him in an acquaintanceship that lasted for decades. It was only when the Yiddish newspaper *The Day* ran a series of articles on Jacob Gordin, however, that Kustan made the connection between his long-standing chess companion and his illustrious father, since Alexander had never mentioned him. He responded to the articles with a few observations about his encounters with Gordin's son, whom he described as someone who

> was always nicely, one might say, elegantly dressed; one would take him for a successful businessman, a banker or a theater director or even for an artist. In addition, he was quiet, polite and well-mannered. How a person with such an appearance could make his living from such a wretched business, and how he could gather pennies from his customers was not something I could understand. And this was already on a grand scale compared to his business in the 'Twenties when in the summer he had a concession for chess in Coney Island on the boardwalk with a few tables where he played for a quarter for every game that he won.
>
> I often spoke with Gordin, but only about chess. He always spoke English. I had the feeling though that he also understood Yiddish. He knew that I was a Yiddish writer but he never with a single word indicated that he too had a connection to Yiddish letters. It was possible that this was because of his retiring nature but also perhaps because he did not want to bring shame on the memory of this father — that his son should engage in such a poor way of making a living. . . . I saw him for the last time in 1954 when he sold his chess place.
>
> An episode in Coney Island is still vivid to me. I remember that it occurred on a weekday morning when I stopped at Gordin's chess table to play with him. I lost the first game, won the second and lost the third. During all the time we played, an elderly woman with a beautiful, one could say aristocratic, face, sat at his right hand holding a shopping bag, seemingly on her way to go marketing. I thought that I saw a strong resemblance between the two, and I assumed that the woman was Gordin's mother. . . . The woman sat patiently throughout our three games. When I stood up and paid Gordin the fifty cents for the games that I had lost, I saw that he gave the woman the money and said a few words to her.

She stood up immediately and left. . . . This scene has always remained engraved in my memory."[35]

In the silence that has ensued, it is hard to reconstruct the clamor, the excitement, the atmosphere of the vast public whose spirits were nourished and entertained by the Yiddish theater in its brief existence. If we include the brave epoch of Maurice Schwartz when the Yiddish-speaking public in America was already in decline, one can reckon the heyday of the Yiddish theater as barely more than half a century.

But the Holocaust wiped out the reservoir of Yiddish speakers in eastern Europe. In America, with its population of six million Jews, Yiddish did not survive as a colloquial language past the first generation of immigrants. The few enclaves where it is still spoken are only among the ultra-Orthodox Jews in Israel and America. Since secular literature in general and the theater in particular are forbidden to these communities, the grand repertoire of old Yiddish plays lies unattended, waiting for an audience. Various brave companies in America and elsewhere attempt revivals with supertitles, and the proliferation of Judaic studies in the universities ensures that some of the names will be remembered.

Gordin's meteoric career is unique in its enormous influence for two decades and in its equally sudden eclipse. This translation of *The Jewish King Lear,* one of his earliest but also most popular works, should give the contemporary reader some sense of the flavor of his plays: their earnestness, their high-minded devotion to principles, and their utterly secure representation of the Old World that was even then vanishing.

Reading *The Jewish King Lear*

When Jacob Gordin wrote his *Jewish King Lear* in 1891, he was working in two firmly established traditions. There was an older line leading back to the Jewish Enlightenment that sought out every opportunity to advance the cause of rationalism and science while denigrating the superstition and backwardness of contemporary Jewish religious practice. And then there was the newer practice in the Yiddish theater of adapting plays from the European repertoire. *Lear* emerged from the confluence of these trends.

Shakespeare's *King Lear* had one particular element that would appeal to the new young Yiddish theater audience in America—their need to consider and reconsider the right relationship between the generations, particularly between a powerful father and the duties of his children. Gordin made an election, as it were, from the rich possibilities of Shakespeare's *Lear*, but it reflected his audience and his own passions.

The Roots of Gordin's *Lear*

As Shakespeare wrote it, the aged Lear decides to relinquish the burden of rule, imagining that he can divide his kingdom among his three daughters, while retaining the titles and profound reverence that had always been his due. When he asks his daughters to tell which loves him most, his two older daughters compete eagerly and sycophantically to spread compliments before him. The youngest, most beloved child, Cordelia, nobly refuses to participate in the competition and is punished for her obstinate silence by exile from his house and his heart. An additional penalty is the loss of a suitor for her hand, who will not take her without a dowry, but his place is instantly supplied by the King of France, who honors and values her more without a marriage portion than if she had come bearing a third of Briton with her.

Lear proceeds to set up his court at the house of first one daughter and then the other and finds he is no longer welcome, no longer honored. By the third act only three members of his large entourage remain: his fool, who tells him unwelcome truths and is still faithful to the banished Cordelia; his old friend the Earl of Kent, who also tells him unwelcome truths, is exiled for it, and returns doggedly to serve him in disguise; and the Duke of Gloucester, who like Lear is tragically blind to the true merits of his children. Gloucester falls prey to the machinations of his wicked bastard son, Edmund, and foolishly banishes his virtuous son, Edgar. Gloucester's loyalty to Lear is punished horribly when his eyes are put out at the orders of Lear's cruelest daughter. Blind and helpless, he is succored by the honorable son he had wronged, while Lear, driven mad by anguish, is rescued by his youngest daughter. The wicked ultimately perish, but too late: Cordelia has been hanged, and Lear dies of grief, while a somber Edgar ascends the throne, surrounded by the fallen bodies of the noble and treacherous alike.

This harsh tale has always been painful for the audience, denying us the relief of seeing justice done and goodness rewarded. As Samuel Johnson put it in 1765 in his magisterial edition of Shakespeare's works, the death of Cordelia is "contrary to the natural ideas of justice, to the hope of the reader." When the English theaters reopened after the Restoration in 1660, only forty-four years after Shakespeare's death, the play had fallen into profound disfavor. In 1681 the playwright Nahum Tate devised an ingenious revision, transforming the play into a love story between Cordelia, Lear's virtuous daughter, and Edgar, Gloucester's virtuous son. Tate eliminated the fool, with all his poignantly accurate insights, and concluded the play with a joyful King Lear blessing the union of Cordelia and Edgar, while Edgar intones the moral, "Truth and Virtue shall at last succeed."

So successful was Tate's comforting adjustment of the play's ending that it swept Shakespeare's original play from the stage. From 1681 to 1838 there is not a single recorded instance of a production of the Shakespeare text, while Tate's work was performed throughout the English-speaking world. As Johnson explained the matter, "The public has decided. Cordelia, from the time of Tate, has always retired with victory and felicity."

When Gordin drew on Lear as a vehicle for his *Jewish King Lear,* he looked back to the original text, recreating the Fool in the person of Trytel. He gave the blunt integrity of Kent to the plainspoken, clear-sighted Yaffe, investing him as well with the romantic tenderness of the King of France, who values his beloved all the more as she becomes less valued by her father. He fused the blinded Gloucester with Lear himself and softened the vindictive treachery of the wicked children into more commonplace sins: Gitele is weak, Moyshe is a drunk, Etele and Avrom Harif are guilty of selfishness and hypocrisy and of a cruel indifference to their old parents' most basic need for food. But there is none of the flamboyant wickedness of Shakespeare's villains in the dismally quarrelsome foursome.

But Cordelia — Gordin's Cordelia, the beautiful and virtuous Taybele — fuses the two heroines into one, one who possesses the strength of character of Shakespeare's doomed princess and the victorious felicity with which Tate crowned her. She has, as well, characteristics which neither Shakespeare nor Tate could possibly have envisioned: she has an education, professional credentials, and real competence in the world outside the tangled conflicts of the family. She is, in other words, an Ibsenite New Woman.

Gordin's representation of Taybele looks forward to the developing theatrical conversation of August Strindberg, Henrik Ibsen, Anton Chekhov, and George Bernard Shaw, and the new theater of naturalism. Naturalism was originally based on Emile Zola's contention that the key influences on man — and hence on the characters of his plays — are heredity and environment. Drawing on the biological determinism of Charles Darwin and the economic determinism of Karl Marx, the theater of naturalism rejects the conventional formulaic plots and morally satisfying conclusions that had hitherto ruled the nineteenth-century theater and instead examines characters with a pitiless, almost clinical eye, displaying them to the audience as creatures of instinctual drives, not in control of their own destinies, devoid of power to change their lives.

Gordin's naturalism, however, was closer in spirit to the more positive flavor of Ibsen's *A Doll's House* (1879); in this play the heroine turns her back on the patriarchal institutions which have shaped her life, walks out of the home in which she is more a child than an adult participant in her marriage, and slams the door behind her. The sound of that slamming door reverberated through the theater for decades, creating in its wake scores of "New Women" demanding the right to shape their own lives. They wanted, as Taybele puts it, to be useful, to lead lives which had value and were not merely ornamental. Shaw created a scandal with one of these New Women in *Mrs. Warren's Profession* (written in 1893, but not performed until 1902); she is a successful brothel-keeper and an unwitting Ibsenite in that she pragmatically reorganizes prostitution so that women can reap the benefits of their labor. James Barrie, who worshiped so devotedly at the altar of motherhood in *Peter Pan,* paid tribute to the New Woman in his one-act comedy *The Twelve-Pound Look* (1910), in which a woman buys her freedom from an oppressive husband by earning her own living as a typist; the price of the typewriter, twelve pounds, is the price of her self-respect. And in the first American Ibsenite play, James Herne's *Margaret Fleming* (1890), the heroine, like Nora, learns with pain that her husband is not the godlike creature she has adored and redefines the sexual morality of the time by taking his illegitimate child into her own home to raise. These three themes — the defiance of convention, the self-respect derived from labor, and the willingness to see clearly the faults of a beloved male authority figure — are the cornerstones of Gordin's Ibsenite revolution: in the character of Taybele, we see them all.

Taybele stands at the crux of the play. In Gordin's neatly designed moral diagram, she is the center; on one side of her, the side of the old, religious world, her father sinks, while on the other, the new, rational world, her husband rises. Her love and loyalty go to both of them, and it is through her agency that the two opposing men are brought, finally, into harmony with what Gordin saw as the new world order.

The Text of the Play

The text translated in this volume is Gordin's own, original manuscript of the play from 1891, a holograph document complete with revisions and second thoughts and lacking only the final page of the text. There is no record of any performance of this original text; there is no printed text, no fair copy, no prompter's script, or any working drafts whatsoever. There are, however, a number of fair copies and working texts extant from 1894 on of another version of this play, a shorter, simplified version, including a text from 1898 printed in Warsaw. A copy of the 1898 text now in the YIVO Library in New York evidently belonged to Jacob Adler, the famous

actor who first played the title role and who achieved extraordinary re-
nown in the world of Yiddish theater for his heartrending performance.
His script is marked by marginal lines that seem to denote cuts; it is clear
that Adler imposed his own reading on the part and it can be surmised that
Gordin's more complex text was revised into the simpler, probably more
stage-worthy version of the drama that Adler played to such success. The
performance text of this play omits the climactic final scene and the Purim
players and simplifies much of the dialogue. Bypassing Gordin, Adler
wrote one of the most famous lines of the play: Dovidl's pathetic appeal, as
he leaves at the end of act 3, "Alms, alms, for the Jewish King Lear!"
Reportedly, Adler's performance of this heart-wrenching moment drew a
shower of coins from the audience as the curtain descended on the old
man, turned out into the world to beg his bread.

A Reading of the Play

The most potent theme Gordin derived from Shakespeare's *Lear* was the
powerful, devastating reversal of the roles of parent and child. A king
relinquishes power and finds that he has been so diminished that his
own children assume mastery over him; even his beloved, loyal, devoted
youngest daughter has mysteriously been transformed and is his child no
longer. In *The Yiddish King Lear,* Dovidl laments bitterly his loss of parental authority and chafes at the humiliation to which he is subjected by the
daughter and son-in-law whom he has made trustees of his fortune. He
rejects even the loving support of his youngest child, Taybele, who returns
to his house as an accomplished, educated woman who can provide him a
home, as he had once provided it for her.

For Gordin's audience of Yiddish-speaking immigrants, this theme
would have been extraordinarily rich. Like every immigrant generation,
displaced between the land of their birth and their adopted country, Gordin's audience was raising children who were far more assimilated than
their parents. The English-speaking children had a competence, linguistic
and otherwise, in the new world that reversed the dynamics of authority in
their parents' home. Just as Taybele seeks out a real education and in the
process learns to reject the assumptions of her parents' house, so Gordin's
immigrant auditors were learning with every passing day that in the new
world they no longer retained the authority they had enjoyed in the old.
And the children of immigrants were learning the corresponding lesson,

that America offered all sorts of riches to those willing to cast off the old and embrace the new.

Act 1: The Rich Man's Table

As the curtain rises, the audience sees a richly furnished room, a table lavishly spread with food, and Khane Leah, the mistress of the house, fussing anxiously over her preparations. "Now it seems to me that every- thing is ready," she tells us and implicitly invites the audience into the play, into the Purim celebration. Gordin deftly lays down the plotlines: the comic servant mockingly chants the rhymes of a wedding jester, the beau- tiful unmarried daughter shyly begs her mother to invite her poor teacher to join the feast, and the servant steals some raisins from the challah — not out of hunger, just for mischief. The stern father is hinted at, and the audience seems to have the simple outline of a familiar plot sketched in for them: the humble suitor in love with the rich man's daughter, while the comic servant mocks their maneuvers. With the entrance of Yaffe, how- ever, we realize this is a very different play indeed. His breezy confidence, his dry wit, his astringent view of the Purim celebration all seem to sweep the fusty conventions aside and invite us into the world of rational dis- putation.[1] His poverty does not dismay him: his intellectual riches give him, rather, the air of a prince among commoners. Khane Leah shows him the beautifully risen Purim loaf, adding a superstitious adage, "May no evil eye harm it," as she does so, and Yaffe in response honors the bread but condemns the superstition. To him the Purim story, the Megillah which is read every Purim, is part and parcel of the Jewish experience of "fanaticism and delusion," while the bread represents the solidity of practical life. "Jews! The more Purim bread, and the less Megillah, the healthier it will be for you," he says. The admonition is Gordin's, of course — Yaffe is the playwright's spokesman — but his confidence in offering it, in his shabby clothes, standing surrounded by the splendor of Dovidl's wealth, tells us whole volumes about the world that Gordin is inviting his audience to experience. The implicit invitation of Khane Leah's opening line, to enjoy the pleasures of the rich man's table, is superseded here by a new invita- tion, to enjoy the spacious freedom of the rational mind.

Yaffe's celebration of the goodness of the bread resonates, of course, with an immigrant audience made up of people who worked hard for their daily bread, who knew what hunger was, and perhaps more significantly knew the fear of hunger. In this opening scene, the table covered with rich food and the dialogue peppered with invitations to eat and drink, the audience is being offered a glimpse of a paradise of plenty. This glimpse makes the following acts all the more painful: the bare table and scanty food of acts 2 and 3 remind us of the banquet in act 1. Trytel's hunger, his constant begging for food, which provides an obbligato throughout the middle acts, seems all the more pathetic because we remember how light-heartedly he pilfered raisins and enjoyed his brandy in act 1.

As the stage fills, Gordin shows us a neat diagram of Jewish disputation: Moysheles' two sons-in-law represent the two chief branches of Jewish thought. Avrom Harif, the husband of the oldest daughter, Etele, is a Misnagid, committed to Torah study and the minute observance of fine distinctions, while Moyshe, married to Gitele, the middle daughter, is a Hasid. Hasidism was a more personal, intuitive, mystical Judaism and stressed exuberant celebrations, with singing and dancing. Moyshe and Avrom Harif use their ideological differences as weapons in their struggle for superiority as the Moysheles' sons-in-law. Etele and Gitele similarly quarrel and snipe, the four of them making up a comic background to the larger, graver division between Dovidl's devout Judaism and Yaffe's rejection of superstition in favor of rationality. The true debate in this act and echoing throughout the play is not the puerile sniping of Misnagid and Hasid, but the conflict between narrow-mindedness and fanaticism, on the one hand, and modern rationalism, on the other: as Yaffe puts it, between Megillah and challah.

But the quarrels are stilled as Reb Dovidl makes his majestic entrance. Trytel hushes them all in agitation as Dovidl approaches: he enters, crying, "Gut Yom Tov!" and bringing the holiday in with him. With his entrance the entire mood of the play changes: the comic sparring is over, replaced by formality as his grandchildren rise and greet him ceremoniously. He also brings the audience a reminder of the wealth by which he controls the family: he hands out gold coins as gifts to the grandchildren and diamond jewelry as gifts to his daughters. He invites the family to join him in singing and, as he sits at the head of the table, welcomes his guest, Yaffe, the "heretic," the man who sits with an uncovered head surrounded by his fellow Jews in their yarmulkes.

And here begins the first of many power struggles between Dovidl and Yaffe, between old Jew and new Jew. Dovidl invites his guest to put on his hat—to cover his head in the traditional Jewish fashion—so that the two men can drink a toast together. When Yaffe hesitates about the hat, Tay-bele begs him to put it on, and Yaffe does so, graciously assuring his host, "For your sake, putting on the hat is also not hard." But it is clear here that it is Taybele's appeal, rather than Dovidl's invitation, that has reached him.

The next power struggle is between Dovidl and Taybele, and the point at issue is a larger one; Gordin has moved from matters of custom to ques-tions of value. Dovidl offers Taybele her Purim gift, a diamond brooch. When she, unlike her sisters, fails to express rapture at his gift, her father attempts to win her thanks by telling her the cost of the jewel, suggesting that she is too young to know how to value it. He alternately storms at her and coaxes her, first ordering her back to her place, then relenting and pleading tenderly for her love. "You don't like the brooch? I will buy you a more expensive one, a more beautiful one." He is torn between seeing her as a child, too young to know a jewel's value, and as an adult, too old to be taught how to behave. But when she responds, her response is unmistak-ably that of a woman who has learned a very different lesson from that of submissive gratitude. She rejects the gift *because* of its cost. Lest we miss the true point of her rebellion here, Yaffe makes it clear that her new position is part of his philosophy. Addressing Reb Dovidl, Yaffe argues,, " "How many poor people we could make happy with that money which is squandered on these unworthy stupidities." And Dovidl notes bitterly, "Now I understand where Taybele gets her wisdom. She is quoting her rabbi's Torah. . . . she no longer has her own will."

Dovidl's daughters and sons-in-law chime in obediently, each in turn sycophantically echoing his scorn and criticizing Taybele for her excessive education; as Etele puts it, "Taybele was taught too much, with teachers and music lessons and other useless trifles," but as the cacophony of their blame reaches a crescendo, Dovidl dismisses them all. "They are all cows," he points out to Taybele. "They all do just what I demand of them. And you have more sense than all of them. You are right. Why do you need adornment when God himself adorned you with beauty, with cleverness, with a clear conscience? Give your old father a kiss." Reconciled with Taybele, he invites Reb Yaffe to drink with him, pointing out, "I love a clever and honorable man, even if he is a heretic."

But even in this moment of reconciliation we see the seeds of the next conflict, the real conflict underlying the apparent disputes. Dovidl wishes to retain the true authority over his daughter and over his household. "You will all do only that which I demand," Dovidl says. "If I say that it is day, you must also say that it is day. If I say that it is night, then it must be night." Pliantly, his children all agree, and peace seems to reign. But with each successive test we see the same pattern: Dovidl seems to yield, but in his yielding asserts more power, more control. He forces Taybele to drink brandy against her will and then to make Yaffe sing for the group. As the evening progresses, the conflicts become more serious. While the sons-in-law pursue their dispute between the ways of the Misnagid and the Hasid, Yaffe mockingly asks whether God is a Hasid or a Misnagid. Dovidl berates him for his mockery and then commands him to remain at the table.

"You command me!" Yaffe responds incredulously. "What can command me is only my own mind. If my mind commands me, I can do anything in the world!" Yaffe describes his privations as he abandoned traditional Jewish learning and pursued a more secular course of study. "If my mind tells me that I must now suffer hunger, want, cold in order later to arrive at a goal, then I will do it." As the two men thunder at each other it is plain that the mise-en-scène with which we were originally presented — the poor suitor and the rich man's daughter — is misleading indeed, for it is the poor suitor who is rich in confidence and who contemptuously rejects the rich man's table, and the rich man who is paradoxically forced to plead. "Stay here, I'm telling you!" Dovidl cries. "Taybele, don't let him go. I don't want him to go away from here feeling offended."

The Purim players arrive; their play is particularly witless, and once more Yaffe speaks in Gordin's voice. He rejects their crude comedy and berates Taybele for remaining in the audience. Once more, Taybele accepts Yaffe's judgment over her father's; once more, her father is left with the plain demonstration of Yaffe's ascendancy over his daughter's will.

It is at this moment, when Taybele's filial obedience has plainly slipped away, to be replaced with a very different allegiance, that Reb Dovidl makes his great announcement. He dismisses the Purim players and announces to his family that he has decided to travel to the Land of Israel and to spend the rest of his days in the study of Torah and in prayer. His two older daughters and their husbands respond with enthusiasm to the notion that he will divide his wealth among them. Their excitement rises to a comic pitch when Dovidl announces that his fortune is a magnificent 310,000 rubles: Avrom Harif's eyes flash; Moyshe Hasid drunkenly spouts Gematria, the mystical numerology that finds divine meaning in the sum of 310,000 rubles. But Khane Leah, Dovidl's old wife, foresees that they cannot count on their children's generosity as easily as Dovidl imagines. Once more, it is Taybele and Yaffe who oppose his will. Taybele rejects the wealthy dowry her father has allotted to her; she does not wish to marry some suitor selected for her but wants to go to St. Petersburg with Yaffe to study medicine. And she does not trust Harif, under whose supervision her father is leaving her. As Dovidl orders her out with Shakespearean rage, Yaffe rises to invoke the name King Lear and to point out to Dovidl how he, like the old king in Shakespeare's play, is dividing his kingdom and banishing the loving daughter who tells him the truth. As Yaffe leaves the stage Dovidl is left with his old wife and his foolish servant, who both see very accurately what a dark future lies ahead of them. The act ends with Dovidl, still in authority, for the last time giving orders in his own house. "Dance! Dance, children! Be merry and joyful!" But only Moyshe and Trytel take up the invitation.

To Gordin's audience, Taybele's banishment would have derived a very special meaning from the setting of the play on Purim. The story of Purim is the story of a tyrannical king who banishes his beautiful wife, Vashti, when she refuses to do his will. He selects another wife, Esther, the heroine of the story, who by her wit and with the guidance of her cousin and mentor, Mordechai, persuades the king to foil the machinations of the evil Haman, who is planning a terrible pogrom on all the Jews. In Gordin's *Lear*, Dovidl is clearly the tyrannical Ahasuerus, and Taybele is at once the rebellious, banished Vashti and the clever young Esther. Yaffe, of course, is Mordechai, who teaches Esther how to speak to the king and through her saves the Jews from annihilation.

The play fits the Purim story perfectly, with one exception. There is no Haman, no true villain in the play: the quarrelsome sons-in-law, the daughters who are either selfish or weak, are not truly evil. They are ungrateful, they are greedy, they are heartlessly indifferent to their parents' needs, but they are not the villains of the Purim story. The enemy, we are to understand, is not any one person, but rather the fatal proclivity to choose ignorance rather than knowledge, frivolous baubles rather than the useful life, pointless doctrinal disputation rather than true learning, Megillah rather than challah. This tyranny of small-mindedness and outmoded custom is the true villain of the piece.

Act 2: Hunger

To Gordin's audience it would have been apparent that the two central acts of this play mark the ascendancy, respectively, first of the Misnagid and then of the Hasidic son-in-law. Avrom Harif, Etele's husband, controls the

Moysheles' house and fortune during act 2, and Moyshe Hasid, Gitele's husband, stages a coup toward the end of act 3. Gordin depicts the two branches of Judaism as two varieties of limited, supersititious thinking. Harif is coldhearted and hypocritical; Moyshe Hasid is weak, self-pitying, self-indulgent. Harif uses his quotations from the sages to conceal the appalling reality: he has abandoned his aging parents-in-law to starvation and misery, first in Eretz Israel and then in their own home. Moyshe Hasid similarly uses his drunken musings on Gematria and Kabbalah to retreat from the real issues that, Gordin argued, transcended speculative minutiae. In act 1, when Yaffe bitterly condemns the Jewish enthusiasm for coarse comedy, Moyshe attempts drunkenly to make sense of the matter by consulting Kabbalah, a compilation of the esoterica of Jewish mysticism: "We will see what foolishness is according to the Kabbalah. Elul is a fool, Chsul is a fool, Petai is a fool. . . ." There is no wisdom to be found in consulting the Kabbalah, Gordin is telling us. Moyshe and his Kabbalah, Harif and his sages, seem intellectually puerile next to Yaffe and his blazing commitment to an enlightened education and a rational mind. Neither Harif nor Moyshe Hasid has any real competence or effectiveness in the world: unlike Dovidl neither of them knows how to make the business prosper, and under neither of them is the household marked by the good will and ample hospitality that characterize the house of Dovidl and Khane Leah in act 1 and of Taybele and Yaffe in act 4. Misnagid or Hasid, the table is bare.

The Purim story begins and ends with feasting, and so does Gordin's play. But between the feast of act 1, when the wealthy Dovidl welcomes the poor Yaffe to his table, and the feast of act 4, when their positions are reversed, we have two heartrending acts in which we see Dovidl fall from mastery to beggary. As the curtain rises on act 2, the scene is the same room in Dovidl's house in which the Purim holiday had been celebrated, but it becomes obvious that matters have changed profoundly. The atmosphere of wealth, ease, and festive welcome is here replaced with weary labor, resentment, and hunger. Dovidl and Khane Leah are now anxious dependents where once they were master and mistress.

What we are seeing here, in act 2, is a representation of the turn of Fortune's wheel. The wheel of Fortune, with the wealthy and powerful riding high on top and the poor suffering below, is an extended metaphor running through Shakespeare's *Lear;* his king, like Dovidl, unwisely sets in motion the events which lead to his own fall, only to find that those who rose as he fell subsequently fall in their turn. "The wheel has come full circle," laments the villain, Edmund, as he lies dying at the end of the play. In Gordin's play the bare table and shabby clothes at the beginning of act 2 suggests the fall, while the general dilapidation we see in act 3 confirms that the terrible wheel is continuing in its remorseless course. As Dovidl says, "I was a rich man and made myself a pauper. I was once a clever man and have turned myself into a fool. I was an honorable man and have become a shame to Israel, so that there is not a moment when I am not sinning before God." He himself set the wheel turning and, with his wife and servant, is now suffering the consequences.

As act 2 opens Trytel, looking older and more poorly dressed than he had during the Purim celebration, is wearily trying to soothe a baby to sleep, as he offers the audience a catalog of woes. "May it not befall other Jews," he philosophizes, as he describes his diminished condition. The comforts and pleasures he had enjoyed as Reb Dovidl's steward are all remembered sadly as he describes the hard work he does now for Etele and her husband Avrom Harif and complains how Etele grudges him food. At first the audience may not fully credit his complaints — we have seen him, after all, cadging treats and brandy in act 1. But then Khane Leah enters with Etele, and we find that she too is peremptorily saddled with chores. Khane Leah must mind the baby; in spite of her failing eyesight she is to mend clothes and sew buttons. And finally Reb Dovidl returns from the Besmedresh, the House of Prayer, looking much older and poorly dressed. "I'm fainting away with hunger," he tells his wife. "I haven't had anything to put in my mouth today."[2]

For Gordin's audience hunger was not a symbol, a metaphor, a figure of speech. These were people with a practical understanding of the harshness of poverty. Even those who were prosperous knew the *fear* of hunger, the awareness that poverty might not be very far away. An illness, an unwise business decision, a dishonest partner or any of a thousand unlucky turn of events could wipe out a family's security. An immigrant, by definition, has left family and friends behind, has ventured into a world where he has to build credit and capital from the beginning. Gordin's audience could not, of course, look forward to programs such as Social Security to protect them from an impoverished old age. In showing them how easily an aging couple could sink from wealth to destitution, taking their loyal servant's fortunes down with them, Gordin was presenting them with a vividly drawn image of everybody's deepest fear.

It is not only hunger but remorse which torments Reb Dovidl; it was his decision to turn over his fortune to his son-in-law, Avrom Harif, and his decision to trust to Harif's honor for his support in the land of Israel. He is reproached, implicitly and explicitly, for his unwise decision, by his wife's tears and weariness, his servant's shabbiness, and most of all by Gitele, who voices what everybody else thinks. "You've left us in good hands!" she cries out sarcastically to him. "In good hands! We'll have you to thank forever!" The ironic form of her resentment echoes the sycophantic thanks she and her sister and brothers-in-law heaped upon Dovidl in act 1. Now that he is poor, there is no more flattery. Now, it is suggested, we see her true thoughts.

"Remind me at every moment of what foolishness I engaged in," mourns a remorseful Reb Dovidl. "I have earned it all; earned it all." And when Etele at long last grudgingly offers him a radish and a roll, he pushes it away. "I have already had enough, my daughter. I have already had enough." The repetition of these expressions, "I have earned it all" . . . "I have already had enough" convey whole volumes of bitter self-knowledge.

It is into this scene that Taybele and Yaffe enter, to take their leave as they head off for St. Petersburg. During the absence of her parents in the land of Israel Taybele had left their house to study and become a teacher. Now, she and Yaffe are to leave the Jewish community entirely, to study medicine among the gentiles. Reb Dovidl blames himself, but paradoxically he blames her more. Even though—or perhaps because—she and Yaffe were right and he was wrong, he upbraids her for disobeying his orders to remain with Harif and for seeking a future among "gentiles and heretics."

But it is clear to the audience that, just as Reb Dovidl's place on the wheel has slipped down, so Taybele's and Yaffe's are rising. Although they are poor now, their ambitions are large and their determination is great. She has come to claim some of the money her father had set aside for her; she wants it not for a dowry, as he had intended it, but as a stipend to support her while she studies medicine. When Harif, who now controls the money, contemptuously refuses it, she and Yaffe are as determined as before to continue as they had planned. "We will both work hard and earn what we need to live," Yaffe tells her encouragingly.

Taybele had left Harif's guardianship, she tells her father, "to study and to work." She wants "to be a useful person." There is a very sharp distinction between the outcome of her studies and those of Reb Dovidl. Although he went to the land of Israel to spend the rest of his days in devout study and although he now spends his days in the House of Prayer, he is no longer a "useful person." He can no longer support his wife in comfort, can no longer see to the proper management of his affairs, and no longer has a voice to be listened to. He has become invisible where he was formerly honored. "No one recognizes me any longer for a father," he complains. "No one asks my wishes. Dovidl Moysheles is no more. Although he's still alive, you've buried him."

But it is clear that the Reb Dovidl who acted with such authority in act Iis still there, diminished less by his unwise trust in Harif than by his own willingness to punish himself. Tortured by the petty squabbles, the meanness and self-righteousness that animate Harif and Etele, he prepares to flee once more to the House of Prayer, until Harif self-importantly demands from Trytel acknowledgment that he, Harif, is the head of the household. This claim brings Dovidl back to life, arousing in him, briefly, the authoritative figure he was at the beginning. "You thought that I was already no more than a broken shard," he roars at Etele and Harif. "You thief, you. That one could walk all over me, spit on me like an old, worthless rag. Hypocrite! Betrayer! You want to know who is here the master of the house? Here, I am the master of the house! I! Reb Dovidl Moysheles! And stand up from your places when I speak to you!" He demands the keys back from Etele and triumphantly reclaims all the property he had given away, property to which he is still entitled under Russian law.

And then, having momentarily cowed his daughter and son-in-law, he throws the keys back at them, scorning to use the loophole that the secular law allows. "I will not permit myself to use such a law. Dovidl Moysheles does not take back that which he once gave away as a gift. . . . My word is dearer than 360,000 rubles!" Contemptuously, he returns all his property to Harif, noting bitterly that Harif has the right "to drive us from here, to draw our blood, to starve us to death."

Once more we have returned to the theme of hunger. "Reb Dovidl has not had anything to eat today," Trytel explains. "He is passing out from hunger." And Harif seizes the face-saving excuse that it is only hunger that has led Reb Dovidl to roar and thunder so terrifyingly. "And that's why you are angry with us, Father-in-law, because of such foolishness as food." But Reb Dovidl, like the audience, sees through the hypocrisy of the argument that food is a foolish matter. Only those who have plenty to eat can afford to scorn hunger. The hungry know there's nothing trivial about hunger.

Act 3: "A Vivat for King Lear!"

Five years pass between acts 2 and 3, five years in which Taybele and Yaffe work, study, become doctors, and finally return home to earn prosperity as "useful" people. As act 3 opens we are still in Reb Dovidl's house, where the furniture has grown even more shabby, and Trytel is mournfully rocking a cradle and singing a song about the turn of the wheel. "The world spins like a draydel," he laments; "Today, a rich man, a wise man, ahero; Tomorrow, a pauper, a simpleton, a zero." His song continues, chronicling the turns of the spinning world from happiness to misery, from strength and riches to absolute zero. The cyclical nature of the rise and fall echoes not only the trope of Fortune's wheel, but more specifically the draydel game that would have been familiar to Gordin's audience. The draydel is a four-sided top with a Hebrew letter on each side. The players play for money, taking turns spinning the draydel rather as one might throw the dice in a craps game; depending on which letter is uppermost, the players may collect some, or half, or all the coins in the pot — or may lose everything. It is the arbitrariness of the game that makes it so cruel a symbol of the fateful wheel; there is no skill involved, only the demands of the draydel. And it is to this song that Taybele enters and is struck, first of all, by how old Trytel has become.

Trytel's tearful greeting to her sums up his discontents: "I eat plagues and curses, and wash them down with worries and illnesses." Taybele reflects on all the hard, bitter days they have lived through — herself as well as her parents and Trytel, but it is clear her passage through the hard times has been upward, from poverty to achievement: she is now "a doctor with all the particulars," as Trytel admiringly describes her. For her father and mother the passage through the five years has been entirely downward. Her father is old, sick, blind, supporting himself with a cane; his first words, as he enters, are "Khane Leah, I want to eat."

Act 3 achieves its effects, its pathos and brief violence, by presenting a very exact contrast — a direct reversal — of the scene laid in the same room in act 1. The busy activity that opened the play, as Khane Leah bustled to make sure that the feast was sufficiently splendid, is here replaced by anxiety at how little there is to eat. In act 1 the whole household waited in anticipation of the arrival of Reb Dovidl, the master of the house. Here only his wife and Trytel give any thought to his hungry existence; where formerly he was the center of the household, he is now barely clinging to the fringes and by the end of the act has left the house entirely.

Whereas in act 1 Yaffe was the outsider, the scorned "gentile," it is now Taybele who is scorned in the same words; it is Taybele who condemns religious superstition and demands bread for her parents. She has successfully achieved her goal, to become a useful person, as we see when she goes to treat Gitele's ailing child. But more significantly, she has reversed the power relationship in the family: whereas formerly she expressed herself hesitantly, knowing that her newly acquired views would offend her father, now she is utterly fearless. To her older sister she speaks commandingly, "Can it be that you're not giving our father food? Give him something to eat right now!" When she learns that Etele has locked up all the food, she becomes a virago, breaking open the locked doors. "What are you talking about — locked up? Break open all the locks! Tear open the doors! He is not only our father, he is the actual lord and master and giver of all this. Serve him food immediately!"

This whirl of angry activity leads to little benefit for Reb Dovidl: amid the noisy confusion of Etele's angry self-defense and Harif's scolding, Reb Dovidl's hunger goes unappeased; there is no nourishment for him in this house. He rejects Taybele's urging that he and Khane Leah come to live with her, still reproaching her bitterly, not only for her own acts, but for the entire catalog of sins of which his children have been guilty. He has been deceived by the "pious and honorable" children, he points out, with biting sarcasm, and so how can he believe Taybele, "a lady philosopher, a nihilist, who is stuffed with worldly wisdom!" More significant, however, is his pride in his own opinion: "I am not changing my mind!" he insists. "I don't change my opinion!" His stubborn will is all he has left, and he clings to the decisions, however wrongheaded they were.

This willful blindness, this determination to cling to convictions which have been proven false, stands in Gordin's play for all the superstition and fanaticism he loathed. Dovidl's pride prevents him from rejecting the false assumptions of his past and reshaping his future more wisely. His rejection of Taybele's bounty at this stage, like his rejection of the property ownership the law afforded him, is not a mere plot device to ratchet up the pathos. Far from it: Dovidl's stubbornness exemplifies the Old World resistance to a new, more enlightened tradition, and Gordin was deter-mined that his audience should see how foolish, how literally blind, his hero was for choosing the wrong path.

For Dovidl does choose the wrong path, in spite of knowing quite well which way he ought to have gone. Perhaps the bitterest element in Dovidl's self-reproach is his self-awareness: he has come to understand entirely Yaffe's argument that he is the Jewish King Lear, now that it is too late to act on it. "I used to think that I saw and understood everything better than others. God has shown me that a little dog that's three days old sees more than me, more than Reb Dovidl, the wise man, the rich man, the hero!" In his blindness, he is aware of how little he truly understood in the days when he could still see. Now, he mourns, "I only now see myself, my own unjust world. The outer world, however, has vanished from me, become dark forever, forever!"

Taybele, speaking to him from a loving heart but also from the ac-quired expertise of her medical training, assures him that she can restore his sight but just as he had rejected the insights that Yaffe offered him in act 1, he rejects her entirely. She made a fool of him, he declares resentfully. Just as in act 2 he rejected the redress the law offered him, to restore his fortune, so he rejects the hope of restored vision that Taybele has given him. In both cases rescue is literally within his grasp; he pushes Taybele away from his embrace, as he had contemptuously discarded the keys to the house, because in his pride he would rather suffer the consequences than claim the recompenses that are offered to him.

Act 3 ends with neat symmetry, as Reb Dovidl's second son-in-law, Moyshe Hasid, invades the house with his Hasidic comrades: in a drunken echo of Taybele's command to break open the locks, he commands his comrades, "Help yourselves to the bottles. . . . In that room, all locked up, there's cherry brandy. Break open the locks and bring everything here. Today I am the master of the house! I, Moyshe Hasid." In savage revelry they seize Avrom Harif and Etele and beat them; the wheel of fortune has turned once more, casting Avrom Harif and Etele down and briefly elevat-ing Moyshe Hasid. When they turn on Reb Dovidl, who is baffled and appalled by the noise and violence, the blind old man turns his back on Taybele and Yaffe, who seek to rescue him, and calls for Trytel. "You are my one true friend," he tells his servant. "Nothing but curses and shame and want here. . . . In this house, they are beginning to beat me."

Reb Dovidl seizes Trytel's hand and commands him to lead him out into the street: he will beg for alms and live on charity rather than starve in his children's house. Trytel loyally insists on coming with him. With an echo of the biblical Ruth and Naomi he cries, "Wherever you are, there am I! Whatever will happen to you, that will also happen to me."

As they leave, Khane Leah appeals to Reb Dovidl, as though he were still a man of wealth and authority who could protect her. "In whose care are you leaving me?" she cries out in dismay. Reb Dovidl urges her to go to Taybele, the beloved youngest child whom he has just so cruelly rejected. "She is an honorable and fine child," he says; his pride won't permit him to accept her love, but he has perfect confidence in it, all the same.

As he leaves the house, the old man has defiantly seized control of his fate once more. Fallen to the bottom of Fortune's wheel, he is no longer a passive victim of his heartless children but is once more governing his own destiny, no matter how impoverished. In the Adler production, this scene was a heartbreaker: he leaves the house beaten, crying out for alms. By contrast, as Gordin originally wrote it, he leaves with head held high. There is a flavor of adventure and fresh confidence in Reb Dovidl's words, as he sends Khane Leah off to Taybele's house. "I, however, with Trytel, will travel a little through the world, and we'll teach ourselves some sense. In a fortunate hour — Reb Dovidl begins a new life." Far from begging, he commands respect. "Respect! Respect! Make way for King Lear!" Old and feeble, he can barely stand but leaves the stage "striking loudly with his stick," Gordin tells us, and shouting "A vivat for the new, for the blind King Lear!"

Act 4: The Wheel Has Come Full Circle

Act 4 marks the most dramatic difference between the play as Gordin wrote it and the play as it was produced. As Gordin wrote it, act 4 included two scenes: the first, set in Yaffe and Taybele's house, is a celebration that closely parallels the festive Purim scene in act 1. The second scene, however, was a very different matter: set in a surgical operating room, it offered the audience the spectacle of an operation to restore Dovidl's sight, performed in silence, while a Catholic Mass is sung offstage. This entire scene was excised from the performance text: as Adler played the part, Dovidl ends the play, still blind, still pathetic, with the promise of restored vision made but not yet realized. Gordin, however, swung the wheel full circle and ended the play with Dovidl's sight fully restored. With his vision restored he acquires as well a confident awareness of right and wrong, of the follies of superstition and the excellence of reason, and he delivers a magnificent speech to that effect.

As the curtain rises on act 4, we seem to have been transported back to the beginning of the play. The room is different — we are in Yaffe's and Taybele's house now — but once more the table is set for a feast, and once more Khane Leah and Taybele are standing together, in festive clothing, preparing for their guests. "Now everything is in its place," says Khane Leah, echoing the words she used as the play opened. Yaffe and Taybele have just been married, and this is their wedding feast. Khane Leah's joy is dimmed by her sad awareness that this wedding feast is very different from the ceremonies she has been familiar with. "Be happy in your own way," she tells Taybele and Yaffe. "I no longer know, Taybele, what to wish you, since you don't reckon as happiness that which foolish and uneducated women treasure." The new world order that Gordin welcomed came with a price, and the most poignant price is paid by a woman like Khane Leah, who is too old to change and grieves for what she misses.

Reb Dovidl is not at his daughter's wedding feast. Two years have elapsed since he left at the end of act 3, and in his absence Yaffe and Taybele have risen in their profession, while Etele and Avrom Harif have fallen a good deal in prosperity. They arrive in the cold and snowy weather of the wedding day to bring a gift to Yaffe and Taybele, only to be greeted by a stern demand, on Yaffe's part, that they make good on their obligations to Taybele and Gitele, that they distribute their share of their father's estate. Yaffe refuses their gift and tells them he is prepared to go to court against them — another reference to the notion that civil authority may appropriately be called in to settle disputes between Jews — and he concludes with the threat of prison against Avrom Harif for his misappropriation of the sisters' portions. Etele points out that the great fortune has been dissipated. "We don't even have a tenth portion of it left. It has all been run into the ground." On this note — poverty, legal liability, familial discord — Avrom Harif and Etele are turned out into the snow, and the true wedding feast commences.

The feast of act 4 closely parallels that of act 1: again there is a speech from Taybele condemning wasteful spending; again there is talk of gentiles and heretics. But now it is mere friendly raillery. Again, just as in act 1, Yaffe is urged to sing, resists modestly, and is finally persuaded, although this time he sings an Italian cavatina. Again there is singing and dancing —

not that of the Purim players, whose coarse entertainment Yaffe had so scorned, but the serenades of the guests.

The serenading includes an odd little game: Yaffe playfully holds the door closed against his Taybele while the guests sing; she cries, "Let me in! Let me in!" as though to remind us of the ghost at the table, the absent father outside in the snow, who should be present with them. As she finally enters, complimenting the guests on the "heavenly singing," she adds, "I can't understand how that has made me think of my childhood and my dear father." Her heart is pained, she tells us, and it is at this bittersweet moment, full of joy and congratulation, and of grief for the absent father, that the little game suddenly becomes a reality. A knock is heard; Yaffe assumes it's a patient, but "every knock echoes in my heart," says Taybele. It is, of course, Reb Dovidl, who has been led to the house by Trytel.

There is still an echo of the old, stern Reb Dovidl in his complaints that "Trytel made a fool of me! He didn't obey me and brought me here — a place to which I had forbidden him to bring me!" But his sternness is covering a keen sense that he has not, in fact, been betrayed. Rather, he himself is at fault. "Do you forgive me?" he asks his daughter. "Will you forgive me? Can you forgive me?" The audience has been yearning for this moment since act 1, and finally gets it. They fall into each other's arms, parting only so that Yaffe can examine his father-in-law's eyes and proclaim that he can cure his blindness.

The scene ends, like act 1, in singing and dancing, but unlike act 1, in which the singing and dancing were a reflection of Dovidl's command, this is a true celebration. All is well, and the company dances for joy.

The conventional story of parted families would end here, and this is in fact more or less where the play ended as it was originally performed. Etele and Avrom Harif arrive, suitably chastened by all their financial and legal difficulties, and forgiveness and general good will finally join the family together again.

Gordin, however, added an additional scene, a brief but powerful one set in an operating room. Yaffe and Taybele together perform the surgery that is to restore Reb Dovidl's sight. As they prepare to begin, we hear the sound of a choir singing a Mass; Yaffe comments what a nuisance it is to have a hospital built right next to a Catholic church, while Taybele is convinced that the singing must be pleasant to a sick person. Against this background the surgery proceeds, and Dovidl's eyesight is completely restored. "The world is once again open to me!" he cries. For Gordin, this is the moment when Dovidl casts aside the narrow-mindedness of the shtetl and embraces the wide possibilities of the Western world. "The darkness will vanish. How dear, how sweet is the brightness of the light."

Dovidl embraces first Taybele, then Trytel, whom he greets as a friend and a brother. "How happy I am," Dovidl says in the exaltation of his restored vision. "I see once again the wide world. I have seen not only the light of the bright sun but also the light of truth!" What is this truth he finally sees? "I was against Science! But look what a wonder science has performed. I thought that a woman had to be dependent on her husband. But look at what a useful person my Taybele is." At one stroke Dovidl has acquired two very different kinds of awareness — both of which, Gordin is suggesting, are part of the same whole. One is the celebration of science — of reason, of the power of the mind, which Yaffe had praised so fiercely in act 1. But the other is the freedom of women to be "useful," to cast off dependency and be a member of the new, rational society in her own right. Both of these new insights coexist in Dovidl's mind with his faith. "Only when a man loses everything with which God blessed him and then finds it again — only then can he judge, can he understand his good fortune! Light! Light! The shining rays of light! Science! True and pure love. Yes! Yes! I believe now that there is pure, holy, true love." Science coexists with faith; in fact, science shows the way to faith, casts a necessary light — the light of Reason — and in that light a man can see clearly what was dark to him before.

Gordin's *Lear* is a parable of the spin of Fortune's wheel — a revisionist parable in which Reason seizes control from Fortune; the rational man need not fear the turns of the wheel, for he takes his destiny into his own hand. As the play opens, the old Jew Dovidl Moysheles is the master of his universe, a universe in which Yaffe, the new Jew, is the outsider. As the play closes, Yaffe is the center, the master, of a new world in which Moysheles is the outsider. Gordin called his play a comedy, not a tragedy, and as he traces the spin of the wheel which effects this change, he shows us why: this is not a tragedy in the Aristotelian sense, the fall of a great man, but a tale of reversal in which one man's fall parallels another man's rise. Moysheles' benevolent good will as he welcomes Yaffe, the outsider, to his house and table at the very beginning of the tale shapes the narrative which takes him by a circuitous route to Yaffe's house, Yaffe'shospitality, and Yaffe's skill on the operating table. By the time the circle closes at the end of the play, all the characters have been around the wheel; all have known wealth and poverty, love and desolation, and the world is beginning anew, Gordin tells us, under a new dispensation. Taybele is the vital instrument in this change: her move from her father to her husband — from the old Jew to the new Jew — demonstrates for the audience that one may cast off the ancient patriarchal tradition for the new rationalism without failing in filial duty and love to the parents left behind. The new Jew, Gordin is showing us, abandons Megillah for Challah and thereby brings the best of blessings to old and new, a clear vision of a new world.

Glossary

Baruch haba	"Blessed is he who comes." A term of greeting for a guest.
Besmedresh	The House of Study.
Cavatina	A term from Italian opera for a short song.
Chabad	An intellectually focused branch of Hasidism.
Challah	A rich braided loaf baked for the Sabbath and other holidays.
Crown School	A secular institution created by the Russian government as an alternative to traditional Jewish schooling.
Draydel	A four-sided spinning top used like dice in a gambling game.
Eretz Israel	The Land of Israel: a term reflecting its religious significance to the devout, before Israel existed as a political entity.
Gemara	Popularly, the Talmud: biblical exegesis and elaboration.
Gematria	A set of hermeneutical rules for interpreting the Torah, based on the numerical value of the letters.
German Jew	A "daytsh," Gordin's term, means literally a German, but the term referred generally to the modern secular point of view that Yaffe represents.
Gevalt	Literally "force, violence," the word devolved into an all-purpose exclamation with meanings ranging from "good heavens" to "murder!"
Golem	According to legend, a man shaped out of clay and magically endowed with life by the sixteenth-century Rabbi Lowe of Prague; the term is used here as an insult to suggest clumsiness.

Groggers	Noisemakers traditionally used on Purim to drown out the sound of Haman's name.
Groschen	A small German coin.
Gut Yom Tov	"Happy holiday."
Hamantaschen	Literally, "Haman's pockets": three-cornered pastries filled with prunes or apricots, eaten on Purim.
Haroset	A sweet Passover dish of apples, nuts, and wine.
Hasid	A member of the Hasidic movement, founded in the eighteenth century in Podolya by the Baal Shem Tov, prizing spontaneity and devotion in worship over the meticulous observance of the law.
Havdalah	The ceremony marking the end of the Sabbath.
Hoshanah Rabba	The last day of Sukkot, a harvest festival.
Hupah	The wedding canopy.
Kabbalah	The esoteric teachings of Jewish mysticism.
Kapote	The long coat — sometimes made of satin — worn by traditional Jews of eastern Europe.
Kazatzke	A spirited east European dance.
Klezmer	Traditional music for festive occasions.
Kopeck	A small Russian coin.
L'chaim	A toast: "To life."
Machpelah	The king from whom Abraham buys a plot of land for Sarah's grave.
Maidel	A young girl.
Mazel tov	"Good luck." A traditional term of congratulations.
Megillah	The scroll wherein the Purim story is told, read traditionally every year at the holiday.
Mikvah	The ritual bath a Jewish wife takes after childbirth or menstruation to cleanse herself before a return to sexual relations.
Misnagid	A Jew committed to minute exactness in religious study and observance.
Pesach	Passover. The holiday celebrating the Jews' liberation from slavery in Egypt.
Pilpul	Hairsplitting religious argument and exegesis.
Rabbinical Academy	A school on an advanced level teaching both secular and traditional Jewish religious subjects and offering its graduates either teaching or rabbinical degrees.
Reb	A polite term of address ("Reb Dovidl") usually abbreviated ("R. Dovidl").
Shabes	Yiddish pronunciation of the Sabbath.
Shadkhn	A marriage broker.

Shavuot	A holiday traditionally associated with the giving of the Torah at Mt. Sinai.
Shechinah	The female spirit of the godhead.
Shofar	A ram's horn, blown like a trumpet at Rosh Hashanah.
Shtetl	A small Jewish community. "A guest in our shtetl" is an expression of surprise at an unexpected arrival.
Shtraymel	A fur-rimmed hat worn by pious Jews in eastern Europe.
Shund	A term in the theater for blatantly commercial melodrama—lit. "trash."
Simchat Torah	A noisy, festive celebration of the conclusion of the annual reading of the Torah.
Talis katan	A fringed garment worn under the coat by devout men.
Tsaddik	In Hasidism, the spiritual leader around whose leadership a sect forms.
Vay iz mir	Literally, "Woe is me."
Verst	A Russian unit equivalent to .66 miles.
Woman of virtue	An expression from the Psalms, praising the good wife.

Notes

Introduction

1. Celia Adler, *Tsili Adler,* 1:142.

Why Do We Smile?

1. Sorin, *A Time for Building,* 105.
2. Gorelick, *City College,* 123.
3. Rischin, *The Promised City,* 73.

Inventing a Yiddish Theater in America

1. Gorin, *Geshikhte,* 1:165.
2. For an example of one of these memoirs, see Dan Kaplanowicz, ed., *Zikhroynes fun a Nikolayever soldat* (Vilna: B. A. Kletskin, 1921).
3. Shatzky, *Hundert vor Goldfaden,* 23.
4. Zipperstein, *Jews of Odessa,* 131.
5. Gorin, *Geshikhte,* 1:92.
6. Ibid., 1:148.
7. Ibid., 1:194.
8. Mlotek, *Mir trogn a gezang!* 4.
9. Gorin, *Geshikhte,* 2:33.
10. Cited in Greenberg, *The Jews in Russia,* 2:73.
11. Joseph, *Jewish Immigration,* 128.
12. Mintz, "Banished," 94, 98–100.
13. Gorin, *Geshikhte,* 1:237.
14. H. Hapgood, *Spirit,* 116, 118.

15. Rischin, *The Promised City*, 33, 94, 119.

16. N. Hapgood, *The Stage,* 247.

17. Mazower, "The Goldfaden Micrograph," Item No. 1.

18. Celia Adler, *Tsili Adler*, 1:173.

19. Quoted in Zilbercweig, *Di Welt*, 55.

20. Young, *Mayn Leben* , 42.

21. Bessie Thomashefsky, *Mayn lebens-geshikhte*, 210.

22. Boris Thomashefsky, *Mayn lebens-geshikhte*, 341.

23. Quoted in Gorin, *Geshikhte*, 2:103, 104.

24. Sandrow, *Vagabond Stars,* 113.

25. Ibid., 302

26. Bessie Thomashefsky, *Mayn lebens-geshikhte*, 189.

27. Boris Thomashefsky, *Mayn lebens-geshikhte,* 332.

28. Jacob Adler, *A Life*, 316.

29. Ibid., 345.

30. Quoted in ibid., 349.

31. Boris Thomashefsky, *Mayn lebens-geshikhte*, 301.

32. Jacob Adler, *A Life*, 245.

33. Ibid., 283, 299.

34. Ibid., 88.

35. Gordin, *Ale Shriften*, 3:3.

36. Ibid., 3:47.

37. Quoted in Zilbercweig, *Di Welt*, 10, 11.

38. Marmor, *Yankev Gordin*, 56.

39. Zilbercweig, *Di Welt*, 11, 12.

40. Ibid., 17.

41. Kobrin, *Erinerungen*, 1:120.

42. Ibid., 1:123.

43. Bessie Thomashefsky, *Mayn lebens-geshikhte*, 196.

44. Ibid., 196, 197.

45. Metzker, *A Bintel Brief*, 143.

46. Ibid., 121.

47. Kobrin, *Erinerungen*, 1:24, 25.

48. Ibid., 2:157, 158.

Jacob Gordin's Life

1. Bessie Thomashefsky, *Mayn lebens-geshikhte,* 199.

2. Zilbercweig, *Di Welt*, 80, 81.

3. Ibid., 87.

4. Marmor, *Yankev Gordin*, 34, 35.

5. Ibid., 32, 33.

6. Kaplan, *Finding*, 35.

7. Cassedy, *To the Other Shore*, xvii.

8. Ansky, *The Enemy*, xv.

9. Marmor, *Yankev Gordin*, 38, 39.

10. Kaplan, *Finding*, 41.

11. Ibid., 47.

12. Marmor, *Yankev Gordin*, 48.

13. Ibid., 41.

14. Bessie Thomashefsky *Mayn lebens-geshikhte*, 198, 199.

15. Kobrin, *Erinerungen*, 111.

16. Young, *Mayn leben*, 78.

17. Quoted in Rosenfeld, *Jacob Adler*, 324.

18. Young, *Mayn leben*, 79.

19. Gordin, *Der Vilder Mensh*, 28.

20. Quoted in Sandrow, *Vagabond Stars*, 146, 147.

21. Zilbercweig, *Di Welt*, 300.

22. Quoted in ibid., 179.

23. Ibid., 234–36.

24. Gorin, *Di geshikhte*, 2:120.

25. Zilbercweig, *Di Welt*, 262.

26. Ibid., 330.

27. Winchevsky, *A tog*, 38, 39.

28. Gordin, *Ale Verk*, 3:226–27.

29. Ibid., 3:227.

30. Sprengel, *Yiddish Theater*, 177. See also Beck, *Kafka*, 135, 136.

31. Marmor, *Yankev Gordin*, 197.

32. Winchevksy, *A tog*, 110–11.

33. Kaplan, *Finding*, 204.

34. Alexander Gordin, "Introduction," i–xiv.

35. Zilbercweig, *Di Welt*, 139–40.

Reading *The Jewish King Lear*

1. For a discussion of Yaffe's role, see Berkowitz, "'Gordin Is Greater Than Shakespeare': The Jewish King and Queen Lear," in *Shakespeare*.

2. For a discussion of the significance of food in this play, see Prager, "Of Parents and Children: Jacob Gordin's *The Jewish King Lear.*"

Bibliography

Adler, Celia. *Tsili Adler dertseylt*. 2 volumes. New York: Tsili Adler faundeyshon un bukh-komitet, 1959.

Adler, Jacob. *A Life on the Stage: A Memoir*. Translated and with commentary by Lulla Rosenfeld. New York: Alfred A. Knopf, 1999.

Ansky, S. *The Enemy at His Pleasure: A Journey Through the Jewish Pale of Settlement during World War I*. Edited and translated by Joachim Neugroschel. New York: Henry Holt. Metropolitan Books, 2002.

Beck, Evelyn Torton. *Kafka and the Yiddish Theater: Its Impact on His Work*. Madison: University of Wisconsin Press, 1971.

Berkowitz, Joel. *Shakespeare on the American Yiddish Stage*. Iowa City:, University of Iowa Press, 2002.

———, ed. *Yiddish Theatre. New Approaches*. Portland, Oregon: Littman Library of Jewish Civilization, 2003.

Cassedy, Stephen. *To the Other Shore: The Russian Jewish Intellectuals Who Came to America*. Princeton: Princeton University Press, 1997.

Cypkin, Diane. "Second Avenue: The Yiddish Broadway." Ph.D. diss., New York University, 1986.

Epstein, Melech. *Profiles of Eleven*. 1965. Reprint. Brown Classics in Judaica. Lanham, Md.: University Press of America, 1987.

Gordin, Alexander. "Introduction," in Jacob Gordin, *Eyn-akters*. New York: Tog, [n.d].

Gordin, Jacob. *Ale Shriften*. 4 volumes. New York: Hebrew Publishing Company, 1910.

———. *Dramen*. 2 volumes. New York: Internatsyonale Bibliothek, 1914.

———. *Der Vilder Mensh*. Warsaw: Druck N. Staravolski, 1907. Reproduced by the Steven Spielberg Digital Yiddish Library.

——. *Der Yudisher Kenig Lir: drama in 4 akten*. Warsaw: Druck N. Staravolski, 1907. Reproduced by the Steven Spielberg Digital Yiddish Library.

Gorelick, Sherry. *City College and the Jewish Poor: Education in New York, 1880–1924*. New York: Schocken, 1982.

Gorin, B. *Di geshikhte fun Idishen teater: tsvey toyzent yohr teater bay Iden*. 2 volumes. 2te. fargreserte oyfl. New York: M. N. Mayzel, Idisher farlag far literature un visenshaft, 1923.

Greenberg, Louis. *The Jews in Russia: The Struggle for Emancipaton*. 2 vols. in one. Edited by Mark Wischnitzer. New York: Schocken, 1976.

Hapgood, Hutchins. *The Spirit of the Ghetto*. Edited by Moses Rischin. Cambridge: Belknap Press of Harvard University Press, 1967.

Hapgood, Norman. *The Stage in America 1897–1900*. New York: Macmillan, 1901.

Joseph, Samuel. *Jewish Immigration to the United States from 1881 to 1910*. New York: Columbia University Press, 1914.

Kaplan, Beth. "Finding the Jewish Shakespeare: A Family Journey. A biographical memoir." Manuscript, ca. 2004.

Kaplanowicz, Dan, ed. *Zikhroynes fun a Nikolayever soldat*. Vilna: B. Z. Kletskin, 1921.

Kobrin, Leon. *Erinerungen fun a Idishen dramaturg: a fertl yohrhundert Idish teater in America*. 2 volumes. New York: Aroysgegeben fun'm komitet far Kobrin's shriften, 1925.

Marmor, Kalmon. *Yankev Gordin*. New York: Ikuf, 1953.

Mazower, David. "The Goldfaden Micrograph (1897). Portraiture and Formation of a Yiddish Literary Celebrity." *The Mendele Review: Yiddish Literature and Language* 9, no. 7 (June 9, 2005): Item no. 1.

Metzker, Isaac. *A Bintel Brief: Sixty Years of Letters from the Lower East Side to the Jewish Daily Forward*. New York, Schocken Books, 1971.

Mintz, Alan. *"Banished from Their Father's Table." Loss of Faith and Hebrew Autobiography*. Bloomington: Indiana University Press, 1989.

Mlotek, Eleanor Gordon. *Mir trogn a gezang! Favorite Yiddish Songs of Our Generation*. 4th edition. New York: Workmen's Circle, 1972.

Prager, Leonard. "Of Parents and Children: Jacob Gordin's *The Jewish King Lear.*" *American Quarterly* 18 (1966): 506–16.

Quint, Alyssa Pia. "The Botched Kiss: Abraham Goldfaden and the Literary Origins of the Yiddish Theatre." Ph.D. diss., Harvard University, 2002.

Rischin, Moses. *The Promised City: New York's Jews 1870–1914*. New York: Harper and Row, 1970.

Sandrow, Nachma. *Vagabond Stars: A World History of Yiddish Theater*. 1977. Reprint. New York: Harper and Row, 1986.

Shatzky, Jacob, ed. *Hundert yor Goldfaden*. New York: Yiddish Scientific Institute, 1940.

Sorin, Gerald. *A Time for Building: The Third Migration, 1880–1920.* Baltimore: Johns Hopkins University Press, 1992.

Sprengel, Peter. "Yiddish Theater in Prague: Kafka and Jizchak Loewy" in (Juan Insua. *The City of K. Franz Kafka and Prague.* Barcelona, Centre de Cultura Contemporania de Barcelona, 2002).

Thomashefsky, Bessie. *Mayn lebens-geshikhte. Di layden un freyden fun a Idisher star actrise.* (New York, Varhayt Pub. Ko., 1916) Reprint of the Steven Spielberg Digital Yiddish Library.

Thomashefsky, Boris. *Mayn lebens-geshikhte.* (New York, Trio Press, 1937) Reprint of the Steven Spielberg Digital Yiddish Library.

Warnke, Bettina. *Reforming the New York Yiddish theater: The cultural politics of immigrant intellectuals and the Yiddish Press, 1887–1910.* (Unpublished Ph.D. dissertation, New York, Columbia University, 2004).

Winchevsky, Morris. *A tog mit Ya'akov Gordin.* (New York, M. Mayzel, 1909).

Young, Boaz. *Mayn leben in teater.* (New York, Ikuf Farlag, 1950).

Zilbercweig, Zalmen. *Di Velt fun Jacob Gordin.* (Tel Aviv, Farlag Elisheva, 1964).

Zipperstein, Steven J. *The Jews of Odessa. A Cultural History, 1794–1881.* (Stanford, California, Stanford University Press, 1986).